NO-HASSLE HOUSE CLEANING

D0202161

NO-HASSLE HOUSE CLEANING

Christina Spence
"THE HAPPY SLOB"

BETTERWAY HOME
CINCINNATI, OHIO

Other fine Betterway Home Books are available from your local bookstore, art supply store or direct from the publisher. Visit our Web site, www.fwmedia.com.

13   12   11   10   09   5   4   3   2   1

Distributed in Canada by Fraser Direct
100 Armstrong Avenue, Georgetown, ON, Canada L7G 5S4, Tel: (905) 877-4411

Distributed in the U.K. and Europe by David & Charles
Brunel House, Newton Abbot, Devon, TQ12 4PU, England, Tel: (+44) 1626 323200,
Fax: (+44) 1626 323319, Email: postmaster@davidandcharles.co.uk

Distributed in Australia by Capricorn Link
P.O. Box 704, S. Windsor NSW, 2756 Australia, Tel: (02) 4577-3555

Library of Congress Cataloging in Publication Data
Spence, Christina
  No hassle housecleaning / Christina Spence.
     p. cm.
  Includes index.
  ISBN 978-1-55870-881-5 (pbk. : alk. paper)
  1. House cleaning. I. Title.

TX324.S77 2009
648'.5--dc22
                                 2009013837

Edited by Jacqueline Musser; Designed by Clare Finney; Production coordinated by Mark Griffin; Cover illustration and interior pattern designs by Lisa Ballard

About the Author

Christina lives in Calgary, Alberta, Canada, with her husband and two cats. (The cats would like it known that this book would've been impossible without their assistance and encouragement.) This book is the realization of a crazy online dream that came true after Christina worked for years as a freelance writer. Visit the Web site that started this whole journey at www.happyslob.com.

Acknowledgments

I would like to thank everyone who helped turn my dream into reality. My editor, Jacqueline Musser, found me online and has been devoted to this project from the very beginning. Thanks, Jackie, for your patience and guidance throughout this process. I needed it! And a huge thank-you goes out to everyone at F+W Media who were willing to take a chance on me and this book.

To Colin, who makes my heart smile. Thank you for being the truest friend I've ever known. To my incredible parents and to all my family, friends and coworkers who believed in me —and made me giggle—along the way.

Contents

Help Has Arrived!

I love this section's title! It makes me feel like a hero, ready to swoop in on a sponge mop to give you a knowing smile and wink as I take you by the hand and lead you off into the wonderful world of housecleaning.

As the original happy slob, I'm here to guide you through the previously hopeless tasks of cleaning your home. It doesn't matter if you're living in a bachelor apartment or a sprawling ranch house—this book is for you! The techniques and habits you'll learn will help you no matter where you live or how much you used to hate cleaning.

This is going to be a fun, painless and enlightening journey for you. If the situation is dire (such as your mother-in-law heading over to your place right now), quickly—and I do mean quickly—turn to any section in the book for code-red cleaning tips. For instance, if your bathroom is your worry, turn to Chapter 11, and you'll get code-red emergency cleaning tips to help.

Otherwise, take your time to learn these fun new techniques and start implementing them right away. You won't feel overwhelmed or stressed out.

Your home will be tidier, more organized and more serene. By clearing your space, you'll clear your mind enough to get out there and do the stuff that really matters. Your friends will likely notice the difference, and you can just smile enigmatically and tell them you've learned the secret to true serenity.

This is going to be a fun, painless and enlightening journey for you!

Now, let's carry on, troops. This is going to get good...

1

The Happy Slob's Secrets to No-Hassle Housecleaning

REPEAT AFTER ME,

"I am a happy slob and proud of it."

Excellent! If you're holding this book, you've likely recognized your own happy-slob mentality and perhaps felt a stirring of kinship when you read my title (the "Happy Slob") on this book. Of course, as a happy slob, I've tried to surround myself with others of my ilk. Birds of a feather, and all that jazz... Let's clarify: Happy slobs aren't lazy, we're relaxed. We're not unmotivated, we're unconcerned. A happy slob is the kind of person who's always good for a laugh and enjoys relaxing with friends at their side and a glass of wine in their hand. We always prefer to smell the flowers rather than the floral-scented chlorine bleach. To us, life is for the living—it's all about the small, joyful moments we'll remember and cherish forever. It's not about obsessively cleaning our homes, seeking some unreachable level of perfection.

But even we happy slobs need help, as we can be cleaningly challenged. (Take the quiz on page 14 to see if you are so challenged.) Our appealing, laid-back attitudes can get a bit out of hand. When I was a teenager, it was entertaining to let the pizza boxes in my bedroom grow their own fungal accompaniments, even if it did nearly break my mom's will to live. As a young adult, however, it wasn't as cool to have friends or family over to an apartment that truly was a pigsty. It got a bit embarrassing, and I decided there had to be a way for a happy slob like me to clean an apartment with minimal time and effort. Voilà! The 3-Step Solution was born—an easy way to keep my little home clean without a lot of fuss and hoopla. You'll learn more about this simple system later. You are going to love it as much as I do because it's different than anything you've ever read about cleaning. I guarantee it!

IF YOU MUST CLEAN, DO IT THE NO-HASSLE WAY

Relax! Even though you now know conclusively (after our thoroughly scientific quiz) that you're among the cleaningly challenged happy slobs, you also have help near at hand. And you're far from alone—most of us happy slobs haven't a clue how to go about the basic tasks of cleaning our homes because sometimes we just don't see the point. Why struggle and clean when it's only going to get messy all over again?

Ah-ha! That's the secret of *No-Hassle Housecleaning*. You will learn how to clean your home quickly and easily, and you will also learn some handy tricks to keep it cleaner longer, which means you will in fact reduce the overall amount of time you spend cleaning.

Are you cleaningly challenged? Take our quiz!

Has cleaning become one of life's greatest obstacles to you? Do you dread it more than your yearly physical? Find out if you're cleaningly challenged. Ready with your pencil? Answer each question with a TRUE or FALSE.

1. The scent of lemon furniture polish sends me into fits of delight.

2. Who needs hobbies? I'd rather spend my free time cleaning the tub grout with an old toothbrush.

3. I clean because it's a soul-enhancing experience.

4. Washing dishes is more enjoyable than watching my favorite TV show.

5. Doing laundry is a snap. I could probably teach classes on stain removal and advanced laundry techniques.

6. I can't remember the last time I cleaned out the refrigerator. I have some leftovers in there that were fresh when Reagan was in office.

7. Of course I wash the toilets! I flush them, don't I?

8. My shower drain is beginning to look like a hairy, scary science experiment.

9. Dust in my home has become less a nuisance and more a decorating statement.

10. Vacuuming causes noise pollution, and I like to think of myself as quite the environmentalist.

There are no rigid, hard-and-fast rules here—I'm just teaching you some new habits that make cleaning something new and amazing: fun! Yes, I said it—cleaning can be fun. I know, I know, you likely have images of your mother opening your bedroom door and grimacing at the sight within. As you already know, I've been there, too. Maybe in the past we've hated cleaning, but no more!

There are no rigid, hard-and-fast rules here... cleaning can be fun!

You might even come to enjoy it, like I have. Here are some of the main tenets of *No-Hassle Housecleaning*.

Maximum Results in Minimal Time

You will spend minutes, not hours, cleaning every day, and the time is adjustable. You're the one in control of how much time you spend. Maybe your grandma told you it takes hours of housework every day to maintain a perfectly pristine home. She may be right, if you

ANSWERS:

If you answered FALSE to questions 1-5 and TRUE to questions 6-10 (or if the majority were answered in such a way), you can safely say you're a clean-ingly challenged like the rest of us happy slobs!

actually want to live in a perfectly pristine home. But really an ac-cumulated effort of minutes each day will work its magic to maintain a neat—not perfect—home.

Neat and Tidy, Not Pristine and Sterile

A lived-in look is fine because you do live in your home, right? I thought so. I don't want to be a neat freak, so why would I want you to be one?

My goal is not to turn you into some obsessive cleaner who wants to live in a sterile environment reminiscent of an operating room. I don't want you to turn into the kind of person who passes out when they see a dust bunny lurking under the bed. No, this guide will let you embrace your laid-back personality while learning simple habits that will help keep clutter and chaos under control. This guide is not about perfection; it's about enjoying your home more because it is neat and comfortable.

Ditch the Guilt Trips

The best thing about *No-Hassle Housecleaning* is that it's easy to stick to. There aren't any complicated regimens to follow. There isn't any guilt either, because if you miss something one day, you'll get to it another day. Life happens, so you needn't feel guilty about it. *No-Hassle Housecleaning* was written by a happy slob just like you! I'm not here to judge or preach. I'm just here to help. I don't spend hours cleaning my home every day, and I don't suggest you do. With trial and error, I've figured out how to tackle even the nastiest cleaning jobs—like scrubbing the tub or cleaning out the refrigerator—with less effort and way less time.

Reap the Rewards

The weird thing about this cleaning plan is that you might end up (gasp!) enjoying cleaning. There's nothing like housework for relieving stress, and you might have some time to tackle an extra chore once in a while. So if you find yourself yearning to do some extra cleaning, it will be our little secret. I won't tell anyone—except for your mother, who'll be thrilled.

These cleaning tips and tricks will literally change the way you live in your home. Think I'm being overly dramatic? Well, guilty as charged, but in this case it's true—a neater home affects not only how you feel about your surroundings but how you feel about yourself. Once you've gained some control over your messy environment, you'll feel freer to have friends and family over at the spur of the moment. Your relaxation time at home will feel more peaceful once you're free from piles of clutter. And if, like me, you happen to work at home, you'll be more productive than ever!

The neighbors may wonder what all the whooping and hollering is about!

TOP TWELVE TIPS FOR MAKING HOUSECLEANING FUN

No one in his or her right mind actually enjoys housecleaning, right? Isn't housecleaning like a yearly checkup: You hate the idea of it, dread it for days, but then finally force yourself to go through with it because you know it's good for you? Housecleaning no longer has to be comparable to medieval torture or intrusive visits to the doctor's office. I know, I know, you're rolling your eyes, yet I promise you, my fellow happy slob, that housecleaning can be a lot more fun than you've ever known.

Here are the happy slob's top twelve tips for making housecleaning fun. (Use these tips at your own discretion—the neighbors may wonder what all the whooping and hollering is about!)

1. *Music, sweet music.* Cleaning with toe-tappin' music on is like having cookies with a glass of milk—they work so perfectly together you can hardly imagine one without the other. Get some funky music that makes you want to move. Workout CDs are ideal for this.

2. *The trusty timer.* A timer will limit how long you clean and help you get the most accomplished in the least possible time. Knowing there's a set amount of time allotted will keep you focused on the tasks at hand.

3. *Supplies at the ready.* A cleaning kit reduces time and stress—everything you need to clean is right at hand.

4. *Pick a corner.* Choose a corner of any room to start cleaning in and go in one direction until you're done. That's it—that room is finished.

5. *Make it a family affair.* When your family and pals want to get involved in cleaning, cheer them on. Don't become a perfectionist, but rather appreciate and commend their efforts, and you'll have cleaning buddies for life.

6. *Comfy clothes.* Wear cozy clothes and comfy socks (or go barefoot if you're into that sort of thing, as I am) while you're cleaning. If you have long hair, sweep it back into a ponytail so it doesn't get dunked in the bucket or, even

worse, into the dark, grimy depths of the toilet. Comfort while cleaning is essential.

7. *Good is good enough.* I do *not* want to turn you into a perfectionist who walks around with a scowl on your face and white cotton gloves on your hands to check for dust. No, as a cool happy slob, you know that when a job is done, it's done. Don't stress if it's not perfect. Life is never perfect! Pat yourself on the back for a job well done and get on with your life.

8. *Reward yourself.* When you stick with your *No-Hassle Housecleaning* routine, treat yourself with little rewards. Even sitting down with your favorite novel or a cup of tea for some relaxation time should do the trick. While you're cleaning, remind yourself it's only for a limited amount of time, and when you're done you'll enjoy a new magazine, cup of coffee, handful of chocolate chips, etc.

9. *Make it a game.* Okay, I realize I sound like Mary Poppins here, but any job can be fun if you make it fun. Washing dishes can be used as time to dream about your next great vacation or of that masterful novel you've always wanted to write. Tedious tasks are surprisingly relaxing and productive when we creative types use them for brainstorming sessions. Silly things such as folding clothes to music can be hilarious to watch—dance a bit, fold a bit, dance with your shirt a bit, make your jeans boogie-woogie… Who cares, as long as it's fun!

10. *Do a little, achieve a lot.* Lots of regular, small cleaning sessions equal a lot of work accomplished but without being as overwhelming. If you're exhausted and couldn't care less about that monster pile of newspapers growing in the

corner of your living room, just do a couple minutes of tidying up and decluttering. All these small, regular efforts add up to impressive results.

11. **Destroy distractions.** A phone call from Mom isn't exactly what you need when you're in the midst of your morning cleaning burst. Your favorite talk show on television isn't likely going to increase your determination to clean the kitchen cabinets. Destroy distractions by turning the phone, TV and computer off while you're working. Once you've finished cleaning, you can go back to being your regular communicative self.

12. **Take a big breath.** Of fresh air, that is. Opening the windows on a beautiful sunny day is a great way to enjoy the weather, even if you're inside cleaning. Of course, there's always that nasty garden to sort out, so if it's a particularly nice day and you want to work in the garden, go for it. You're a happy slob, remember. These things matter more than perfectly sterile surfaces in your home!

THREE STEPS TO A CLEANER HOME

The 3-Step Solution, my friends, is the core of *No-Hassle Housecleaning*. Once you've mastered the 3-Step Solution, you have indeed become a cleaning master! Later on we'll perform some appropriately regal ceremony to crown you. But for now, here is what it all boils down to.

1. Two *cleaning bursts* every day—one in the morning and one in the evening. (Believe me, it's not nearly as painful as it sounds—in fact, these are fun! My two cats generally chase me around as I do my cleaning bursts and help add

to the jolly atmosphere by chasing after my feet or attacking the broom.)

2. Clean one *focus room* every day for just ten minutes. These rooms are on a simple rotating schedule, so every room will get needed attention over time.

3. A *weekly clean-for-all* is when you get some larger cleaning tasks done or work on tasks you couldn't get to during the week.

That's it. The whole purpose of this system is to help you clean more effectively—without being complicated. Fussy, we're not! Fun, we are! These three little steps might sound too simple to work, but they're not. Implementing them will help you gain control over the clutter and mess that may be holding your home hostage.

Where Did This 3-Step System Come From, Anyway?

You might wonder how this 3-Step Solution was developed and where it came from. When I was in my twenties and working as a wannabe novelist, I realized I had to bring in some sort of reliable extra income. My husband was working, but we definitely needed another income to scrape by (and I do mean scrape by—the whole starving novelist concept is definitely well founded. Oh, how I suffered for my art…).

Fussy, we're not! Fun, we are!

In a moment of inspiration, I decided I would clean apartments. We lived in an apartment building anyway, and I'd noticed plenty of people who trudged off to work every morning looking the worse for wear. Surely those people could use a little help keeping their homes neat and tidy! So I created some cute flyers, stuck them under doors and in no time had two regular cleaning jobs that really did help us out. Any money for groceries was greatly appreciated at that time.

It takes tiny steps to get us a tidier home in a reasonable, non-perfectionist way.

I developed some ideas while I was actually cleaning other people's homes. But the main goal I had in mind was to turn my husband and myself from true slobs to happy slobs—people who would be neater and tidier but not obsessively so. *No-Hassle Housecleaning* was born!

Mama Knew: Pick up After Yourself (P.A.Y.)

There are very few hard-and-fast rules in *No-Hassle Housecleaning*, but one I'd love for you to learn and apply is to pick up after yourself (P.A.Y.). It sounds so simple, right? It truly is a basic idea, and one our poor mothers have been trying to implant into our stubborn craniums for decades. But how often do we neglect this simple advice?

Like any habit, picking up after yourself (or P.A.Y.ing, if you like) takes a little time to get used to. So start right now! P.A.Y. by putting away the pile of travel books you were looking through last night. And pretty much every time you're holding a piece of dirty laundry, it's a good time to P.A.Y! Drop it directly into the laundry basket (or washer itself, if you've got a load of wash ready to go), and there you have it. Good job!

You can't easily P.A.Y. if you don't have a place for these essentials to go in the first place. So during your focus-room cleanings or weekly clean-for-alls, take a little time to analyze how you organize. Think about the tasks you perform day in and day out and the items you use over and over again. The goal is to simplify your daily routine—things should be easy to find, and they should be where you need them right when you need them. A housecleaning notebook might be a handy place to jot down areas that need improvement.

Remember to teach this method to your kids, roommates and family members. Sure, you might sound eerily like your own mother, but don't we all after time? It's absolutely inevitable, so embrace it.

Code-Red Cleaning

Code-red cleaning outlines the quickest cleaning techniques to get your place shipshape *fast* for when visitors are coming. If your mother-in-law (or other scary person) is on her way, or your boss just happened to decide to drop in for a quick chat, this is where you need to turn *pronto*!

Trust Your Timer

Your time is valuable. I know you'd rather be outside in the garden or at the beach or looking chic at the local coffeehouse while reading some fabulous new novel. You'd rather be doing anything besides grunt work like toilet scrubbing and freezer defrosting. I hear you because I wouldn't exactly list toilet scrubbing at the top of my Dreamy

> *What doesn't get done today will get done another day. There's no need to stress!*

Things To Do list either. It's not on the top of anyone's list unless you're a neat freak. And if you were that, you wouldn't likely be reading this book, now, would you? So to ensure your time is well spent when you're using my cleaning plan, you're going to need to invest a few bucks in a kitchen timer. If you have a timer on your stove, great. If yours is a small apartment or house, and you can hear that timer ringing from any room, that will work perfectly. But if you have a larger home, you'll need to buy a separate timer so you can hear it when it rings. It'll be an essential part of your Basic Cleaning Kit.

I have a cute, little green-pepper timer my husband insists looks like a frog, and I take it with me to each room of our apartment while I'm doing my cleaning bursts and the daily focus-room cleaning. Once that little pepper pipes up, I gladly pay heed to the little fellow, and I'm done with that area of cleaning for the day. That's it—when that timer rings, you're done. What doesn't get done will get done another day, and so there's no need to stress about it.

When you're doing your daily 3-Step Solution cleaning tasks, you'll always set your timer. So you don't need to worry about wasting too much time because your timer will be ticking away and will let you know when your work there is done.

CLEANING TERMS

Housecleaning isn't exactly quantum physics, but there are a few cleaning terms I'll use throughout the book that you'll need to know. So as not to confuse you unnecessarily, here are some of the terms you'll encounter as you wander through these pages.

- *3-Step Solution:* This is what I call the simple cleaning system I use every day. Includes two cleaning bursts and a focus room. Once a week you'll do a clean-for-all. That's it!
- *Basic Cleaning Kit:* The basic cleaning supplies you'll need in order to clean effectively.
- *Cleaning bursts:* Nothing painful, I promise you! Again, cleaning bursts are intense little cleaning sessions—one in the morning, and one in the evening—that are the basis of keeping your home cleaner.
- *Clean-for-all:* A once-a-week cleaning that is more thorough and gives you a chance to tackle anything you haven't done during the week.
- *Code-red cleaning:* Tips meant for emergency cleaning situations. If the love of your life is heading over unexpectedly, these are the tips you'll need.
- *Focus-room cleaning:* Every day you'll spend ten minutes in one focus room. This room changes every day and helps you do a slightly more thorough cleaning in these areas.
- *Happy slob:* What you and I are—laid-back people who aren't fussy and who are almost always cleaningly challenged. Consider it a compliment.
- *Homemade cleaners:* Products you make at home, using common ingredients. These can replace harmful chemical products, if you choose. These recipes are featured in Chapter 3.

- **P.A.Y.:** Stands for Pick up After Yourself. It's the easiest way to keep your home tidy.
- **Scrubby sponges:** Sponges with a sponge on one side and a scrubber on the other to help remove muck faster.
- **Timer cleaning:** Using the kitchen timer to keep track of exactly how much time you spend cleaning. This eliminates wasted time!

HOW TO GET STARTED

Getting started really does begin with good intentions. Read this guide and start when you feel ready. But don't procrastinate—choose a day to begin and then stick to it.

Start with one cleaning burst a day for one week. Then add the second cleaning burst. Once that feels nice and natural, add the daily focus room for a few minutes a day and then work your way up to ten minutes a day. Finally, add the weekly clean-for-all. Beginning with small, new habits makes your new cleaning routine easier to stick with.

Remember that small, consistent efforts add up to big results.

I look at it this way—if you wanted to eat healthier, you wouldn't jump in all at once from eating burgers and fries every day to eating tofu with a side order of wheat berries at every meal. It takes tiny steps to get us where we're going—a neater, tidier home in a *reasonable, non perfectionist* way. If you're going to stick with my happy slob's way of cleaning, do it at your own pace, for heaven's sake. Remember that small, consistent efforts add up to big results. Plus you'll be learning new habits all along, which makes cleaning feel less torturous.

Now, on to those goodies that make cleaning easier—fantastic supplies!

2

Super Supplies

Okay, so maybe cleaning will never excite you as much as bungee jumping or the reality TV shows you're secretly addicted to. (Wow, let's hope housecleaning never gets that exciting! I, for one, couldn't handle it.) But you know what? Cleaning is easier when you're armed with one important thing…

THE BASIC CLEANING KIT

This isn't rocket science. A cleaning kit isn't full of magical cleaning formulas that do all the work for you while you sit back on the sofa with your feet up. (Wouldn't it be lovely if it did? If this guide provided that information, it would surely sell millions of copies!) But I did promise you simpler cleaning, and that begins with a well-stocked Basic Cleaning Kit.

Why is it so important to take the time to create a cleaning kit? Think of all the time you waste hunting around your home for just the right sponges—you know, those cool scrubby sponges we happy slobs love. Or, if you can't find your favorite bottle of cleaner, you'll waste more time searching for that. This is time that could be better spent starting—and finishing—your cleaning. Right now you're likely wasting valuable time hunting for cleaning supplies. But no longer!

A cleaning kit doesn't have to be fancy. This *is* a cleaning kit, after all, not an impress-the-cute-new-neighbor kit with all the essentials, such as breath spray and volumizing mousse. Your cleaning kit has all the stuff you need to get on with the business of cleaning. It is an absolute necessity for anyone doing the 3-Step Solution. What do you need to start compiling a kit? First of all, you need a container to store all the essentials. Otherwise you just have a pile of cleaning stuff in the middle of the room—not terribly helpful to the cause.

Your new cleaning kit will be your constant companion on this trek.

Keep it Contained

Cleaning kits can come in all shapes and sizes. Just use whatever you have on hand for now—plastic storage boxes, an old toolbox, a big cleaning bucket, an oversize ice cream bucket or even a heavy-duty carpenter's apron to stash all the goodies so you can wear your kit instead. A container with a handle is ideal, as it makes carrying the kit easier and therefore increases the chances you'll actually use it. I have an oversize red, rectangular bucket, which is my cleaning kit of choice these days. The handle makes it easy to tote and the shape and size make it just right to hold all my cleaning stuff.

No matter what it's housed in, your new cleaning kit will be your constant companion on this exciting trek into home cleaning. You can even name it if you like. It's beyond me why my cleaning kit has gotten labeled as Betsy, but she has. Once you start talking to your cleaning kit, however, you may have gone a bit too far. But bond with it because this kit will be an enormous help to you in all your cleaning tasks. It can even become your dancing partner while you're waltzing around between tasks. Now explain that to your nosy neighbors!

SUPPLIES CHECKLIST

You've found something to hold all your cleaning supplies. Good! Now you need to go about filling it.

Mini Cleaning Kit Project

Create a miniature cleaning kit or a child's personal cleaning kit by taking a clean plastic milk bottle and cutting off the top, leaving the handle intact. This mini kit is also handy to keep tucked under each bathroom sink for fast and furious cleaning jobs. You can go so far as to decorate the outside, which is especially fun for kids. They can paint or stencil or decorate it however they like. And, of course, the children should write their names on them in indelible ink so the kits' owners can be identified at a glance.

What You DON'T Need

Don't waste your money on loads of specialty cleaners meant exclusively for one job. Very few of those are necessary for us no-hassle housecleaners. Most of the cleaning-kit supplies listed below are multitaskers—saving you time and money. You also have the choice between using commercial cleaners or homemade cleaners. (Homemade cleaners are easier on your wallet and your health because they use natural, readily available ingredients.) Chapter 3 contains recipes for all the different types of cleaners you'll need for your cleaning kit.

What You DO Need

1. *A notebook and pen or pencil.* This is a must for no-hassle housecleaning. On your daily cleaning bursts, you'll jot down problem areas to target during the weekly clean-for-all. You can also mark down when you need to restock essentials such as sponges, white vinegar, baking soda or paper towels.

2. *Sponges, cloths and paper towels.* Sponges are great for wiping up all sorts of surfaces, but I especially love scrubby sponges—a regular sponge on one side and a scrubbing pad on the other. You can buy them in bulk packs at dollar stores or find them in any supermarket. Cloths are a frugal cleaning choice because you can pop them in the washing machine and use them over and over again. (Old shirts, tablecloths, worn-out jeans, etc., can be ripped apart and used for just this purpose. Don't bother buying cleaning rags except for a few microfiber cloths.) Paper towels are useful for many purposes, such as if you're wiping off the toilet and would rather just throw that icky mess away.

3. **Microfiber cloths.** These are a new obsession of mine because they can simplify your cleaning. These cloths leave an absolutely streak-free shine on glass and mirrors that even we happy slobs can admire! Plus, microfiber cloths won't scratch delicate surfaces such as photographic or computer equipment.

4. **Newspapers.** These are excellent for cleaning windows and mirror because they don't leave smudges and lint behind.

5. **Old toothbrushes.** These are handy-dandy little cleaners for scrubbing hard-to-reach nooks and crannies.

6. **Garbage bags.** For tossing out trash or storing stuff until you can deal with it later. Recycle whatever you can before throwing it away. I also like to keep a selection of smaller, plastic grocery bags in the kit to sort clutter.

7. **Static-electric duster.** For easier dusting around the home. Feather dusters just molt their feathers all over the place like wacky birds, so use this or use clean white socks on each hand and go crazy dusting with both hands! That's an especially fun task for the junior happy slobs amongst us.

8. **Rubber gloves.** For the messier jobs and for whenever you're using harsh chemicals. They help protect your hands and make you look like a very serious housecleaner indeed.

9. **Broom and dustpan.** To get the dirt off the floors. What did you think they were for?

10. **Scrub brushes.** Especially helpful for cleaning floors or bathtubs, or for various other cleaning tasks.

11. **Baking soda.** Buy a lot of this miracle cleaner because this is a no-hassle cleaner of choice. It's useful in about a million and one ways (at least!).

12. **White vinegar.** Buy just as much of this as you did the baking soda because it's every bit as useful. This powerhouse does everything from cleaning coffeepots and showerheads to softening clothes and boosting dishwashing power.

13. **Spray bottles.** Clean spray bottles will be useful to you when you make your own simple cleaning formulas, starting in the very next chapter. Don't reuse bottles that have contained nasty chemicals. Instead, just invest in a few new vest in a few new spray bottles that have adjustable spray nozzles. (My two favorites both came from the dollar store, so you definitely don't need to invest much!) And if they happen to be in cute, cleaning-inspiring colors, all the better.

Baking soda is useful in about a million and one ways (at least!).

14. **A "shiny" cleaner.** Shine it up with either a homemade or a commercial window cleaner. My favorite is the Very Vinegar spray. (You'll find a recipe for it in Chapter 3.)

15. **A "gritty" cleaner.** This gritty cleaner scrubs grime away. You can choose between a natural type and a commercial product. Good old baking soda is my gritty cleaner of choice. Just store it in a spice shaker for easy dispensing.

16. **A "germ killing" cleaner.** A disinfectant you can use wherever you need to get rid of all sorts of nasty little germies. Again,

your choice, but natural options such as tea-tree oil or white vinegar do a fantastic job.

17. **A "soapy" cleaner.** Good old liquid dishwashing detergent. Choose a mild, natural type whenever possible. There are more biodegradable options than ever—just check at your local supermarket.

18. **A "degreaser" cleaner.** This is helpful on surfaces prone to grease buildup, such as in the kitchen. Lemon oil is a wonderful natural option that smells delicious.

19. **Wood polish.** To shine up your precious wooden furniture. Keep a lint-free cloth wrapped around the bottle just for the purpose of polishing wood. Again, good natural options exist that use real, essential oils.

Extra Goodies

While not strictly essential, these handy extras make life a lot easier when you're learning how to clean the no-hassle way.

- **Sweeper mop.** I love these! Basically eliminating the need for a broom, dustpan, mop and bucket, these sweepers with replaceable cloths will sweep up the muck on your floors. Or use the wet cleaning pads to mop the floors with ease. You can use heavy-duty paper towels instead of the refills—they won't work quite as well, but they're cheaper. Or, if the thought of dumping these refillable sheets into the landfill fills you with dread, try some of the environmentally friendlier options—you can purchase washable and reusable refill pads instead. When you're done mopping, you can rinse off the pad and then chuck it into the washing machine.

- *Motorized bathroom scrubbers.* These things are amazing! Absolutely, immorally lazy, of course, but if you hate scrubbing the tub and tiles, they are a godsend. They come with replaceable scrubbing heads that do all the work for you—you just have to click on a switch. These are especially handy for anyone with mobility issues who finds getting at the nooks and crannies of the tub difficult.
- *Carpet sweepers.* These little darlings are inexpensive, lightweight and very handy for sweeping up small messes on floors and carpets without dragging out the heavier-duty vacuum cleaner. They also don't scare cats, by the way. (My cats are terrified of the regular vacuum cleaner.) If you don't have a vacuum or can't afford one right now, spend a few bucks on a carpet sweeper instead.
- *Carpet cleaners.* If you have one, great. It takes out the cost and hassle of having to borrow or rent one of these. You can even go halvsies with a friend, split the investment cost and share ownership of it.

3
Homemade Cleaning Recipes

It's your choice: homemade versus commercial cleaners. Some of you simply won't have the time or inclination to make lovely homemade cleaning products. But let me do a little convincing: Most of the recipes in this book take a few seconds to put together. The ingredients are seriously inexpensive, and they are easier on your health and the environment.

But if you really love your regular cleaning products, don't stress about it. Go ahead and keep using them. (Just don't spend loads of time and money shopping for luxury cleaners—they simply are not necessary. The cheap cleaners work just the same as the higher-priced cleaners.) You can carry on to the next chapter. I'll see you soon!

If, on the other hand, you do want to try whipping up some of your own formulas, this section is for you! You're going to have fun trying these simple, effective recipes. Once you've tried these, you'll never go back to commercial cleaners.

Making Your Own Cleaners

I'm not the type to carry on with a lot of scary statistics about how commercial cleaners will destroy your health, your wealth and all your brain cells, but for some of use using natural products isn't an option, it's a necessity. If you or anyone in your family suffers from allergies or any serious health ailments, using natural cleaners is the only choice.

I have a friend who has such severe allergies that if I wear anything scented (even clothes washed in regular laundry detergent) she'll get viciously sick for days. Sadly, these ailments are becoming more and more common nowadays, making natural cleaners more necessary than ever.

For frugalites like myself, basic homemade cleaners can also save a lot of hard-earned cash. With a few basic pantry essentials, you can whip up all sorts of effective cleaners for just pennies, especially if you buy the ingredients in bulk.

The Antibacterial Debate

Anything antibacterial sounds like a happy slob's best friend. If it kills bacteria, it must be good to have around, right? Not necessarily. In fact, research has proven that these cleaners actually increase the resistance of bacteria—in effect creating superbugs that are harder to kill. Plus you're killing the healthy bacteria along with the nasty stuff, and healthy bacteria are good for us. Regular old soap and water—for cleaning both your home and yourself—is all you need. Just choose a natural cleaner that uses white vinegar or plain soap.

INGREDIENTS CHECKLIST

Here are the basics you'll need to whip up any of the following formulas whenever you need them.

1. **Baking soda** (sodium bicarbonate). It does more than just bake, baby! Baking soda is useful in literally hundreds of ways around the home. It's a nonscratching powder cleanser and a natural air freshener, too.

2. **Beeswax** helps solidify a mixture, usually to use for waxing and polishing. It has a lovely, sweet scent.

3. **Borax** (hydrated sodium borate) is a naturally occurring mineral compound found deeply embedded in the ground with other substances such as clay. It makes an excellent powder cleanser and gets whites whiter in the laundry.

4. **Club soda** helps blot out the nastiest, darkest stains on your carpets. Best to use right away before the stain has a chance

✳Essential Oils

Essential oils not only smell great; they are natural cleaning powerhouses. Feel free to add a few drops to your favorite cleaning recipes. Here are the properties of some common household essential oils:

- **Eucalyptus oil**—disinfects
- **Lavender oil**—disinfects
- **Lemon, orange and grapefruit oils**—degreases
- **Lime oil**—degreases and is a general cleaner
- **Pine oil**—disinfects, degreases
- **Tea-tree oil**—disinfects and is effective against mold and mildew

to settle into the carpet fibers. It also shines up appliances and countertops—in my opinion, better than any commercial "shiny" cleaner you can buy.

5. **White vinegar.** It's a natural acid, so it does the job that many of those harsh acidic cleaners do but without harming you or the environment.

6. **Salt.** Another essential that is inexpensive and very common. The grit helps wipe all sorts of nasty stains away.

7. **Citrus juices.** Orange and lemon juices are excellent cleaners and degreasing agents. An extra bonus is that they smell absolutely delicious—like a refreshing summertime punch.

8. **Plain toothpaste.** Not the gel type, but regular old toothpaste. Great for certain cleaning tasks. A cheap variety will work nicely for cleaning tiles, grout and more.

9. **Oils.** Different types of oils, such as lemon oil, almond oil or olive oil, help shine up certain surfaces and add moisture to finishes. Especially helpful when cleaning wood.

With a few basic pantry essentials, you can whip up effective cleaners for pennies.

CLEANING RECIPE COLLECTION

"Squirt, Squirt" Cleaner

Liquid dish soap (not antibacterial)

Tap water

Our first formula is so quick even the laziest of us happy slobs won't mind giving it a try! Even if you usually don't make your own cleaning products, this one is so ridiculously simple you'll love it, even if only to use when you run out of the store-bought stuff.

Squeeze a couple squirts of natural liquid dish soap (*not* antibacterial, please) into a funky spray bottle and then fill up with cool tap water. Give it a gentle shake, and you have an excellent all-purpose cleaner. And, yes, it is fun to say "Squirt, Squirt" out loud while using it.

Scrubby Cleanser

Baking soda

Cleaning sinks and bathtubs is far easier when you use a scrubby cleanser matched up with a scrubby sponge! Just remember this: "Scrubby gets rid of grubby!"

Baking soda can replace all the powder cleansers in your house! Use on a sponge to work off that grime and then rinse away with water. Store baking soda in a spice shaker, clearly marked, and then it's easy to use for cleaning.

Window and Glass Cleaner

¼ tsp. mild liquid dishwashing detergent

3 tbsp. white vinegar

Tap water

Blue food coloring (optional)

These surfaces are tough to clean because they show every fingerprint and mark. After much testing, this is the formula I love the best for cleaning windows and glass around my place. This one product is truly all-purpose as you can use it on glass or any other surface.

Combine all ingredients in a spray bottle and add a label. Gently shake before each use. The food coloring simply helps you identify the product because most commercial glass cleaners are blue. Use as you would any other window cleaner, and use newspapers to get the windows and mirrors extra clean, minus the streaks and smears. The dishwashing liquid helps remove buildup that commercial sprays likely left on these surfaces. After a few times, you can leave the soap out if you like and just use a white vinegar and water solution.

Window and Glass Cleaner II

Club soda (fresh or stale)

That's it! Pour into a spray bottle and use with newspapers to clean any glass or mirror surface. Very inexpensive, and there's absolutely no mixing or measuring. Good for people who really hate that vinegar smell. You can use this same spray on linoleum floors to mop up easily without using a bucket! Just use a moist sponge mop.

Why does it work? The sodium citrate in club soda softens the water and gets the surfaces streak-free clean. You'll be surprised to see how well this works.

Baking Soda Cleaning Spray

Baking soda

Tap water

Pour one or two tablespoons of baking soda into a spray bottle and fill
with water. Shake well before each use. This makes a great all-purpose
cleaning spray that is simple and incredibly thrifty! You can add a few
drops of your favorite cleaning essential oil if you want a nice natural scent
and more cleaning properties.

Homemade Furniture Polish

3 tbsp. olive oil

1 tbsp. white vinegar

Combine in a bowl and use a soft cloth to apply. Or you can pour this
mixture into a small spray bottle if that makes it easier to use. Dust the
surface first, removing visible dirt. Use a little of the polish on the cloth,
and buff the wood.

Your wooden furniture will sparkle with new life after you polish it
with this stuff. The oil restores wood, while the white vinegar pulls dirt out
of it. Use a soft, lint-free cloth to give it a good buffing. You should be able
to see your gorgeous reflection in the surface once you're done.

Makes a Great Gift

This recipe can easily be doubled or tripled. Bottle it in old-fashioned
glass bottles, and it makes a very nice gift for friends. And they'll be so
impressed to know you made it!

Mighty Tea-Tree Cleaner

1 tsp. pure tea-tree oil

1 cup water

5–10 drops lemon oil (optional, for degreasing)

Derived from the Melaleuca bush of Australia, this powerful oil has been used for centuries as a disinfectant and germicide. This is what to turn to when you're faced with a seriously moldy surface. It's perfect to spray on musty, moldy shower curtains—just spray on and let sit; you don't have to rinse it away.

Combine in a spray bottle and be sure to label. Spray on areas that have mildew or mold, and don't rinse off.

Add five to ten drops of lemon oil to this mixture, and you have an excellent disinfecting kitchen and bath cleaner. The lemon oil adds a pleasant scent and extra degreasing action.

Scrubbing Soda Paste

Baking soda

Liquid dish soap

Tap water

Instead of using commercial liquid cleansers, you can make this simple solution that is convenient to use on tubs and showers in particular. When it's time to clean the bathroom, just whip this mixture up in a bowl big enough to dip your sponge into. Use in the bathroom or anywhere else you use thick liquid cleansers.

Pour a generous amount of baking soda (½ to ¾ cup) in the bowl. Add a few generous squirts of dish soap (whatever type and scent you prefer) and just enough water to create a thick paste. Use full strength on tubs, tiles, toilets and sinks. Rinse with water after cleaning.

Very Vinegar Cleaner

White vinegar

Tap water

A few drops of citrus essential oil (optional)

When a friend told me this cleaner smelled like the bottom of a pickle jar, I almost renamed the stuff. This all-purpose cleaner is excellent for surfaces all around your home, as white vinegar works naturally to kill mold, bacteria and germs. And it's better for us *and* the environment than chemicals or bleach. As for the "bottom of the pickle jar" aroma, don't worry. It dissipates quickly after use, and you can open the windows or turn on a fan if you want the smell gone really fast.

Fill a spray bottle one-quarter full of white vinegar and fill nearly to the top with plain tap water. Give it a good shake before each use. To sweeten the smell a bit (and add degreasing action), you can add a few drops of a citrus essential oil such as lemon, lime or orange.

Carpet Stain Lifter

1 part white vinegar

2 parts tap water

Combine ingredients into a squeeze or spray bottle. Blot up as much of the stain as possible before you begin. (Blot gently so as not to push the stains farther down into the carpet.) Then saturate the stain with the carpet-stain-lifter solution. Cover with a few pieces of paper towel and then add something heavy on top, such as a book, to help soak up even more. You'll likely need to do this a few times to completely remove the stain. Once completely dry, vacuum over the spot to finish cleaning.

Carpet Stain Lifter II

½ cup borax
2 cups water

(For even tougher stains!) Shake ingredients in a squeeze bottle until borax is fully dissolved. Test a small, inconspicuous area of your carpet for color-fastness before you use this cleaner. Borax can have a bleaching effect on carpet fibers. Use the same technique as with the Carpet Stain Lifter recipe.

General Clean's Floor Cleaner

White vinegar
Water

Okay, so there is no General Clean, but I like the name of this floor cleaner because it means business. Don't be surprised to see white vinegar once again in the list of ingredients—the multitasking stuff is a miracle cleaner around the home.

Add about 1 cup of white vinegar to a bucketful of fresh, clean water and use as an all-purpose floor cleaner. The scent of the vinegar will dissipate quickly—just leave the windows open to get rid of the smell even quicker.

✳ Add a Pleasant Aroma

Add a lovely herbal scent to this floor cleaner. Brew a cup of your favorite pure herbal tea and add it to this mix. (Peppermint or chamomile are my favorites.) Add the cup to the solution in the bucket. This is especially nice for spring cleaning!

HOMEMADE SCENTED PRODUCTS

We want our homes to smell wonderful—like fields of flowers in bloom or like bread fresh out of the oven. Better than Dad's sweaty feet and the dogs' chew toys, right? But you don't need to spend a lot of money on commercial air fresheners because you likely already have all the things you need to make your home smell great.

Baking soda is the greatest odor absorber on the face of the planet, which is nice because you don't want to just mask stinky smells, you want them gone for good.

A sprinkling of baking soda in the cat's litter box, or some dissolved in plain tap water and then sprayed in the air as an air freshener, will do a great deal to remove odors naturally. (Just remember to shake the mixture before each use.) This is a wonderful option for people with allergies or serious illnesses, as baking soda is very mild and won't cause adverse reactions. Keep a box of baking soda open in particularly smelly areas (not just the fridge, though it's useful in there, too) to help soak up the nasty smells. Replace the box every couple months. A box of charcoal briquettes also does a good job at soaking up nasty smells and leaving the room smelling fresher. Ah, like a spring breeze!

Lovely Labels

Try making your own custom blends! They make cool gifts when you bottle them in funky spray bottles and label them. You needn't use plain labels either—if you're artistically inclined, you can go crazy with designing gorgeous custom labels. If you aren't artsy, try creating labels on the computer and printing them out.

There's more you can do to make your home smell great besides just removing offensive odors—you can also add great scents. Try simmering a few cinnamon sticks and some whole cloves in a bit of water on top of the stove. You can add some lemon or orange zest to the mix, and it will smell like delicious home-baked cookies. It's a warm, welcoming scent that Realtors claim helps increase the appeal of your home at open houses! Who knew a pantry raid could be so valuable? Homey smells like this really entice visitors to stay in your home longer. You'll feel the same way when your home smells so delectable.

If you want to try your hand at making some natural air fresheners with essential oils, I've included a couple basic recipes. Essential oils are the concentrated oils from natural sources such as leaves, flowers, roots and bark.

Fragrance oils are man-made, synthetic scented oils that cost less but never smell as good as the real stuff. Not only will essential-oil natural sprays make your home smell great, but they have aromatherapy qualities, too. For instance, lavender or chamomile makes you feel relaxed, while citrus oils such as lemon are refreshing and invigorating.

Bottle It

When making these natural sprays, always use a clean spray bottle with a fine-mist setting. Never use bottles that have contained other chemicals—there could be a dangerous reaction. And to protect the potency of the essential oils in the blend, use dark glass bottles such as amber or cobalt. Finish off each spray bottle with a label.

Lavender

Distilled water
Lavender essential oil
Bottle with spray attachment
Label

Personally, I could have a bit of a lavender dependency problem. My friends and family claim I do, but I'm still in denial. Doesn't everyone have a bottle of lavender spray by the bed? And in the bathroom? And in the kitchen? Okay, so maybe I do have a bit of an issue. But who wouldn't? Lavender is a gorgeous herbal scent that helps calm your nerves and soothe your senses.

Fill the bottle nearly full with distilled water and add a few drops at a time of the lavender until you get a strength you like. Add a label and voilà—instant mood maker! Spray on bed linens a half hour or so before bedtime, and you'll sleep like a baby. Also a nice spray to keep in the bathroom.

Vanilla

½ cup distilled water
3 tbsp. pure vanilla extract
5–10 drops vanilla oil
Bottle with spray attachment
Label

A lovely, pure scent, vanilla is said to set the mood for love! Pour all into a spray bottle and shake well before each use. (Make sure the bottle has a fine-mist spray setting.)

Potpourri Sachets for Dresser Drawers

You can add scent to musty closets or dresser drawers by creating simple potpourri sachets. Use any square piece of pretty fabric—old napkins work very well for this—and sew along three edges. Fill with your favorite blend of herbs or potpourri and blind sew the last edge to seal the scented goodness inside. Tuck into any dresser drawers or add a little ribbon hoop on top and hang in any closet. Much nicer than what it smelled like before!

If the scent begins to wear out after time, add a few drops of your favorite essential oils onto the potpourri and shake to distribute. It will add new life to your sachets.

Zesty Citrus

Distilled water
Citrus essential oils of your choice
Bottles with spray attachments
Labels

In aromatherapy circles, citrus essential oils carry many different properties. Lemon oil helps you feel more alert, aware and joyful—a great spray for the mornings. Sweet orange, on the other hand, promotes feelings of sensuality, joy and creativity. Experiment with your own favorites.

Fill the bottle nearly full with distilled water. Add a few drops at a time of your essential oils until you get a custom blend you love. This is a very personalized project to which you can add a few drops of other essential oils.

4

Step One:
Cleaning Bursts

**A *burst of energy* armed
with a few cleaning essentials
equals a cleaning burst!**

Step 1 of the *No-Hassle Housecleaning* 3-Step Solution is cleaning
bursts. The word *burst* makes me think of a spark of energy. So think
of your daily cleaning bursts as energetic cleaning sessions when you
get a lot accomplished quickly.

There's one burst in the morning and one burst in the evening.
Cleaning bursts are when you get to act like a complete fool, dancing
around the house with conveniently placed cleaning supplies close
at hand. It's a great way to zap stress and dirt at the same time. Turn
on your favorite music and get carried away. Finally, cleaning will
become more *fun*.

TWO DAILY BURSTS: A.M. AND P.M.

For most homes, these cleaning bursts will last anywhere from five to fifteen minutes. If you have a tiny bachelor apartment, you'll obviously need less time. If you have a massive mansion, you'll likely need more time. (And if you own a massive mansion, and yet clean that mansion all by yourself, my hat is off to you!) But for most of us a maximum of fifteen minutes will do quite nicely. You can and will adjust this time on a daily basis. *You* decide how much time you need to devote. On a busy morning, maybe you'll have five minutes for a quick cleaning burst. Great! On another day, you might have twenty minutes to spare. It all evens out in the end, and you're the one in control here. There's more to life than cleaning, so you decide how much time you can afford to spend and then stick to it.

Sure, five to fifteen minutes isn't a huge amount of time to spend cleaning, so remember that cleaning bursts are maintenance cleaning activities. Basically, they maintain a tidier home—they don't deep clean that home. For more tips on what you can accomplish in your allotted cleaning-burst time, flip to the next pages for lists of basic cleaning to do in the two major impact areas. (In the next

To Kit or Not to Kit

You don't need to carry your Basic Cleaning Kit with you when doing your cleaning bursts; you can leave it somewhere accessible or just carry along the few essentials you'll really need, such as cleaning spray and a few cloths. Or, if you prefer, a mini kit can easily be created in a small plastic bucket with a handle.

section, you'll also learn more about what impact areas are and how important they are when doing your cleaning bursts.)

For now, think of it this way: The A.M. cleaning burst gets your day off to a great start by leaving the kitchen, bath and living areas tidier. The P.M. cleaning burst gets you ready to face the next day, and that often includes the same areas, plus a little bit of preparation to make the next morning more bearable and not such an exercise in stress!

CLEANING IMPACT AREAS

Impact areas are the areas that you, your family and visitors see and use the most often in your home. Cleaning these areas, therefore, will have the greatest impact on the overall tidiness of your home. The kitchen, living area and bathroom are the impact areas in our place—the areas we tend to live in the most. Figure out what your impact areas are and focus more attention during your cleaning bursts on these areas first. Your list might read like this: living room, kitchen, dining room, main bathroom, home office. Ask your

Take That Timer with You!

To successfully complete your cleaning burst, you'll need a reliable timer. I like a loud-ringing digital timer that is easy to set and use. For maximum portability, try buying one that has a rope—you can hang it around your neck and always know exactly when your allotted cleaning time is up. And it's a mighty attractive fashion statement, to boot.

family which rooms they think are the impact areas in your home. Make sure you hit these areas the most often during cleaning bursts so you never have to worry when visitors pop by unexpectedly. If these most commonly used rooms are kept fairly tidy, you'll never have that heart-dropping sense of dread when friends stop by unannounced and you're rushing around like a madman armed with a broom and dustpan!

There's more to life than cleaning, so you decide how much time you can afford.

The Two Major Impact Areas: Kitchen and Bath

They say kitchens and baths sell a home—and in the case of *No-Hassle Housecleaning*, they also make or break a cleaner home. For most of us these are the two major impact areas in our homes because most everyone sees them and uses them on a daily basis. (Unless you aren't big into eating and showering, in which case... what are you into?) Make sure to hit both—at least briefly—during your cleaning bursts. You'll be astonished at how small but frequent amounts of attention will add up to some pretty impressive results in these areas.

Here are some practical ideas you can use during your daily cleaning bursts in these two most important areas. This information will help you stay focused and give you a general idea of what can be accomplished in your timer-limited cleaning session.

Cleaning Burst Spotlight: Kitchen

Some tasks to include:

1. **Dishes!** In the evening, if the dishwasher is full, start it up before you head to bed. In the morning, it's time to empty the dishwasher so that any dirty dishes accumulated during the day can be popped right in to that most wonderful appliance and not left to linger in the sink. This alone is one of the greatest habits you can get into because once you've tackled dirty dishes, you've taken a huge step toward a cleaner, less cluttered kitchen.

2. **Wipe down counters.** Always keep a clean, fresh dishcloth or cleaning rag ready for this very purpose. (My favorite tip for cleaning a dishcloth so it's always fresh and at the ready: Clean it in the dishwasher! During a regular cycle, simply place the cloth on the top shelf. You can anchor it with a dish if needed. No more nasty-smelling dishcloths!)

3. **Wipe down other surfaces.** The kitchen counters are the most obvious surface, which you already dealt with in step two. But other mucky surfaces in the kitchen need a good swipe

Zap Your Dishcloths

Another fast, fresh way to clean dishcloths (minus soaking them in bleach) involves your microwave. After use, simply rinse off the dishcloth, and then pop it in the microwave on a microwave-safe plate for one minute on high. It kills the nasty germs right away—just be sure not to burn your hand when you reach in to retrieve it!

with a cleaning cloth, too—such as the tile backsplash or even walls. If your eye catches some muck or grime lingering, just give it a quick wipe-down. That grunge and grime is no match for you!

4. **Wipe down appliances.** This needn't be a daily occurrence, but wiping down both large and small appliances on a regular basis really does help them stay shiny and clean. Those appliances you keep out on your counter—for instance, the microwave and toaster—will look far better when wiped clean. So when you have a few moments left before the timer rings, wipe, wipe, wipe!

5. **Clean the sink and taps.** This is just a nice way to finish up. A clean sink—one devoid of all muck and dirty dishes—is a lovely thing to face the next day. It's so much better than a pile of dirty dishes awaiting you when you haven't even had your first cup of joe. The nerve!

6. **Sweep.** A great habit to get into is to sweep at the end of every day. I also like those convenient mops with replaceable cleaning cloths—and every few days I also mop the floor that way. Getting into the habit of sweeping every day will mean so much less of crumby mess later on, and your daily sweep will be a breeze.

Cleaning Burst Spotlight: Bathroom
Some tasks to include:

1. **Wipe down surfaces.** As with the kitchen, surfaces in the bathroom really do well with a quick wipe. I usually wipe down the counter areas and anything that looks a bit dusty or grimy.

2. **Mirrors.** A speckled, spotted mirror just makes the whole bathroom look unloved! (And it doesn't exactly do wonders for our reflections either, does it?) So keep your glass cleaner on hand with either a bunch of newspapers or lint-free cleaning cloths to shine up the mirror quickly and easily.

3. **Toilet.** Again, not exactly an in-depth (no pun intended!) clean, but try for a quick wipe-down with a paper towel and a disinfectant spray. (My favorite is the Mighty Tea-Tree Cleaner recipe in Chapter 3. Tea-tree oil is a real king of natural disinfecting.) This is one time I do use paper towels exclusively because I like to chuck that nasty, germy mess right away.

4. **Sink and faucet.** Make the bathroom look snazzy with just a few swipes of your cleaning cloth by tackling these vital spots. A shiny sink and faucet make a huge difference to the look of your bathroom. Just a few sprays on the faucet with your favorite glass cleaner, and a few swipes, and you're good to go. The sink is nearly as easy—just a sprinkling of baking soda or powdered cleanser and a scrub with the scrubby sponge or scrub pad, and your sink will sparkle. Just rinse it out a bit to get rid of the residue to achieve that lovely shine.

5. **Decluttering action.** The bathroom is another area where bottles, jars and containers just seem to multiply of their own accord. Take back your countertop and surface areas by tidying up quickly and putting things into the medicine cabinet, under-sink storage, wherever. And, of course, teaching your family to put things back when they're done using them is a huge help in controlling the clutter monster.

A Positive Attitude is Contagious!

One of the best ways to get your roommates or family in on the cleaning action (without nagging) is to be positive about your new cleaning routine. You could say, "Isn't it amazing how good the place looks?" or "It doesn't take long to keep our place looking great, does it?" That, coupled with the obvious results of your efforts, will spur them on to help more often. Show them how much you appreciate it when they follow through and really try to clean. Not only will it teach them to help around the house, but it will also help *you* out tremendously!

Pick a Corner, Any Corner

To maximize your allotted cleaning-burst time, pick one corner of a room to start cleaning in and work in one direction until you're back where you started. No backtracking and no worrying about what didn't get done. Once you've come around and reached your starting point, you're finished in that room! Remember, you're practicing these techniques on a regular basis, so if something is missed, you'll find it the next time around. This is maintenance cleaning, not deep cleaning; move as quickly as your body will allow and carry on bravely!

They Really Work

Since I started doing two daily cleaning bursts, our apartment stays remarkably tidier. You're doing this cleaning twice a day, so the results really add up. Don't worry if you can't do a cleaning burst once in a while. It's your home, for heaven's sake, and it won't self-destruct if you go one day without cleaning it. But, as time goes on and you've done more and more cleaning bursts, the overall clutter and mess will be reduced to more manageable levels.

Just try it, starting today, and you'll be surprised at how big a difference such seemingly small efforts can make. And remember, you're not to tackle the cleaning bursts alone—recruit your family or roommates to help and divide up the areas. Top floor to you, lower floor to them. Or divvy up the rooms amongst yourselves, and you'll finish fast.

CLEANING BURST KNOW-HOW

During any cleaning burst, you should be armed with a few cleaning essentials, including cleaner and cloths and a supply of plastic or canvas bags. As you travel from room to room picking up clutter, stuff the clutter into those bags. Carry one bag for each room in the house and place stray items in the bag to be returned to the correct room—kitchen clutter in one, bathroom clutter in another and so on. Deposit those bags in the appropriate rooms at the end of the cleaning burst, and the house will be looking great, and you can deal with that clutter later. (Deal with clutter bags either during a clean-for-all session on closets or during a focus-room cleaning in

Don't tackle cleaning bursts alone—recruit your family or roommates to help.

that particular room. To make sure those bags of hidden clutter don't get forgotten, be sure to add that task to your notebook.)

Also keep a bag of things you'd rather give away than throw away. Many local charities or thrift shops would be glad to have your donations. Your clutter will become something useful and functional for another family who really needs a bit of help. Now, how wonderful is that?

Charting Your Problem Areas

While you're doing your cleaning bursts, keep your notepad and pen handy at all times, perhaps conveniently tucked away in a pocket. When you see a problem area you can't sufficiently tidy up on your short cleaning bursts, jot it down. All these problem areas will eventually get dealt with during your focus-room cleaning and your weekly clean-for-all. And, yes, if you're a high-tech happy slob, by all means use your favorite techie organizer. (That's truly about the extent of my knowledge of such gadgets.) But whatever you choose—low-tech notepad or high-tech organizer gizmo—just keep track of the areas in your home that really need some extra love and attention later on.

A.M. CLEANING BURSTS

Basically, your two daily cleaning bursts will accomplish the same thing—a lot of tidying and sprucing up in a short period of time. But your A.M. cleaning burst will have a slightly different result. Your day is just starting when you tackle your first cleaning burst of the day, so some of the tasks here will help you better face the day. And with the stressful, hectic lives that most of us live, our morning cleaning bursts are a fantastic jump on the day or a way to start the day off on the right foot. It's sort of like eating oatmeal for break-fast—you may not absolutely love it, but you know it's good for you, and it starts off your day in a way that will benefit you all day long. Your morning cleaning burst will start the day off right for you and your whole family, and you'll be *so* glad you did it when you get home later on.

Here are some special hints for your first cleaning burst of the day. These are by no means exhaustive but represent some of the tasks you can do in fifteen minutes or less that make a huge differ-ence to the look of your home.

1. **Dishes**! Again, dishes are first and foremost on the list. A cluttered sink full of dirty dishes is downright depress-ing to face later on when you come home, exhausted from work and facing the idea of throwing dinner together. Clean out the dishwasher every morning and get every-one in the habit of putting dirty dishes directly into the dishwasher. And when the dishwasher is full, get it started right away.

2. **Beds.** Make your bed, missy! Oops, there I go sounding like my mom again. But seriously, another must-do assignment

Less Mess = Less Stress

Sluggish in the mornings? Is cleaning the last thing on your mind? To get motivated, remember this motto: "Less mess equals *way* less stress!" The more frequently you do your morning cleaning bursts, the better your home will look, and the less stressed out you'll be when you return home.

in the morning is to make your beds. And that means all the beds in the house—get everyone old enough to make their own beds in on the action. Anyone who can stand should be making his or her own bed, and that includes three-year-old Timmy. (Tips on bed making made easy are in Chapter 13.)

3. **Clothing and closets.** Just as dirty dishes have an incredibly annoying tendency to gather and reproduce, abandoned clothing does the same thing! Take a couple minutes to gather up discarded clothes that are lying around and put them away in the closet or dresser.

4. **Garbage/recycling.** For many families the morning is a prime time to take out trash or recyclables. If your mate/roomies/ kids are able, this is definitely a great task to delegate.

P.M. CLEANING BURSTS

Just as your A.M. cleaning burst started your day off with a bang, your P.M. cleaning burst will end the day peacefully and get your family prepared for the next day. It's a beautiful cycle that really works—the benefits of your morning cleaning burst mean your P.M. cleaning burst isn't as difficult. And then your efforts at night mean everyone can function more smoothly the next morning, and so on.

The day is nearing its end, and you may already be in your pajamas. (When I do my P.M. cleaning burst, I usually am, complete with fuzzy slippers for comfort.) You're basically setting things right so the morning hustle and bustle will be a little less hassled and harried. Some important things that your P.M. routine might include are:

1. **Dishes!** Do you notice a trend here? Dishes are a biggie when doing your cleaning bursts. Think of it this way—do you want to face that huge pile of dirty dishes in the morning? I didn't think so. So make sure the sink is cleaned out every night or the dishwasher is loaded with dirty dishes. If there's time to do only one task before you haul yourself to bed, make it this one. It's a great routine to get into.

2. **Pick-up six.** You've heard of pick-up sticks—well, this is my version. Pick up and tidy up six things every evening (when your timer allotment allows you). Again, focus on tidying up the impact areas. Let this saying catch on with the family and get the kids and your spouse (or roomie or whomever) to "pick-up six," too. It's a fun cleaning habit to get the kids into before they go to bed. Make it a game, and it'll become a helpful habit that sticks with them.

3. **Wipe down.** It sounds like baby-changing time, but I actually mean to wipe down surfaces in the kitchen and bathroom especially. A quick swipe of surfaces with your cleaning cloth and cleaner will make things look fabulous—fast.

4. **Pet stuff.** Cat litter can be changed as part of a nightly cleaning burst, as can tidying up around the pets' dishes, etc. Nighttime is a great time to handle a few cleaning tasks for our beloved furry companions (no, not you, Uncle Stanley).

5. **Sweep.** As mentioned in the kitchen-cleaning list, sweeping daily is a great way to end your cleaning burst in the evening. If you sweep nearly every day, it's so easy to do! Every few days (or whenever necessary), I also bring out the lightweight mop with replaceable cleaning cloths to quickly spruce up the floors.

GETTING STARTED WITH CLEANING BURSTS

Some people like to jump right into the entire cleaning plan without a backward glance. Others prefer to start slowly, dipping their toes in the water before diving in headfirst. If you plan on gradually implementing your new cleaning routines, this is the place to start. Cleaning bursts aren't intimidating, but they do reap impressive results. And, keeping the happy-slob mentality in mind, they're not so structured as to be overwhelming—you set your budgeted time on the timer (anywhere from five to fifteen minutes, depending on that day's schedule) and get busy cleaning. Start with just one cleaning burst a day and stick with it every day for a week or two until it becomes as much a habit as your cup of morning coffee. Then, and only then, add the other daily cleaning burst. Then you're ready for focus-room cleaning.

5

Step Two: Focus Rooms

Once you've gotten accustomed to doing two cleaning bursts a day, it's time to bring in the focus-room cleaning. Focus rooms are fantastic because the room feels so different when you're done. When you spend ten minutes in any one room, you get an amazing amount of tidying, organizing and cleaning done. The secret to success? Stay focused! That's why I call it a *focus* room, after all.

We happy slobs like to wander about, searching for new or lost treasures all the time. "Ooh, look at that great shirt I'd forgotten I had!" Or "Wow, I didn't know I owned that book—it's really about time I sat down and started reading it. And I do mean right this moment." It's hard for us to remain focused on one task, one idea, one person or one dream. So when I call it a *focus room*, I literally mean that. Be determined to stay focused on cleaning and tidying that room alone. If you find items that belong somewhere else, such as a packet of skewers in the bathroom that should be in the kitchen (unless, like me, you use those handy things to dig out nasty drained clogs), just pop those items in a plastic bag. You'll deposit that bag in the kitchen later on. Keep a bunch of bags in your cleaning kit for this very purpose.

Don't leave the focus room once you arrive. Stay for the full ten minutes. By spending ten minutes a day in a focus room, you'll get a lot of cleaning and organizing accomplished in a relatively small amount of time. When you're done with your focus-room activity for the day, simply plunk the clutter bags into the appropriate rooms (let's say bathroom, kitchen, kids' rooms, etc.) and deal with it later, specifically during your next focus-room cleaning in that room or during the weekly clean-for-all. This isn't just a way to move clutter from one area to another but a way to clean consistently and get items back where they belong.

THE FOCUS METER

It sounds like a complicated element of a high-end camera, but the focus meter is something altogether different. The Focus Meter allows you to rate yourself from 1 to 10 after doing a focus-room cleaning in one room—1 being very poorly focused on that area and 10 being amazingly focused. This may seem silly, but if you catch

✳ Concentrate on Bigger Tasks

Think of focus-room cleaning as cleaning under a friendly microscope, which means you'll want to look at cleaning tasks in each area you wouldn't even glance at in your quick cleaning bursts! This is a deeper clean, getting tasks done you wouldn't be able to accomplish during your regular cleaning bursts alone.

yourself thinking focus-room cleaning really isn't working for you, the problem might be that you just can't get or stay focused. Rating yourself in an honest way will help you work on this important element of the *No-Hassle Housecleaning* methods.

So what if you really aren't feeling focused? Your Focus Meter reading sits sadly at a 5 or less—not really the focus and motivation you were hoping for. That's okay! If you discover your focus was waning, write down why that might have occurred. Something as simple as a distracting phone call or feeling unwell can easily sap our focus and our motivation right along with it. Write down the reason you weren't feeling focused, and over time you'll see what your true distractions are.

If, over time, you see that the same distractions are disrupting your cleaning routines, switch things up! Or, more accurately, switch things off. Phone calls are a biggie when it comes to serious distractions, so if they get you off track, could you turn off your cell phone

Clutter Bags

Clutter Bags isn't your new nickname; it's simply what I like to call the bags of accumulated junk I find in one room that need to be put back in the room where they belong. Keep a stash of plastic grocery sacks or canvas bags with you in your cleaning kit to deal with clutter as you come across it. Deal with this accumulated—but nicely hidden—clutter the next time you do a focus-room cleaning, or add it to a weekly clean-for-all. Make sure to jot down "clutter bags in closet," etc., in your handy notebook so you don't forget about them.

for just ten minutes to destroy that distraction before it destroys your focus? Or, if you're distracted by the TV or a laptop, just turn it off. No matter what your personal distraction, change your routine so you're able to stay focused for the full ten minutes. That time will fly by, and then you can carry on with whatever else you want to do.

If the same distractions disrupt your cleaning routines, switch things up!

And if it's just general lack of interest that's causing you to give up on focus-room cleaning, remember this one important point: It's only ten minutes! You can even chant that to yourself while you're cleaning if it makes you feel better. So even if you never get to the point where you yearn to clean, just think of it as ten minutes to make the rest of your day (and life) run more smoothly. Anyone can endure ten measly minutes if it's for the betterment of his or her life, right? And seriously, a tidier home makes for a lot less stress overall—a thing you'll learn firsthand when you keep using the *No-Hassle Housecleaning* techniques. So set that timer, get to it and try your very best to stay focused.

TAKE OUR TEN-MINUTE CHALLENGE

Will ten minutes really make a difference? Definitely! Ten minutes in an average-size room is a lot of time to tidy up, especially when you can stay focused on that room exclusively. Work on those tasks

> *Anyone can endure ten measly minutes if it's for the betterment of his or her life.*

you don't always do in your cleaning bursts. Look at the top, middle and bottom of the room and see what really needs cleaning and then tackle those jobs. Pretend you're seeing the room for the very first time and try to see it as other people see it—work on those cleaning tasks you don't usually get to. Limit your enthusiasm to ensure you can actually finish the tasks you start within your ten-minute allotment of time. You don't have to get everything done today because you'll have another focus-room cleaning in this room within a week or two.

Still not convinced that ten minutes in any one room can get a whole lot of cleaning action done? Oh, ye of little faith. Well, okay, let me prove the point to you with some action. Better yet, I'm going to let you prove the point to yourself by taking on my ten-minute challenge. Take out your trusty kitchen timer and set it for ten minutes. Beforehand, work out a little plan of action. Let's say you want to work on your master bathroom today—that glorious, spalike sanctuary you like to hide away in amidst a great bubbly bath. Your goals might look something like this:

- Clear clutter from countertops.
- Get rid of ten pieces of junk from the medicine cabinet or storage beneath the sink.

- Clean the light fixture.
- Give the toilet a thorough cleaning.
- Clean the accumulated dust and grime off the fan vents.
- Wipe down some of the walls (if time permits).

That looks like a whole lot of cleaning work to do in just ten minutes, right? Well, the amazing thing about focus-room cleaning is that if you can stay truly focused on the room at hand, you can accomplish more cleaning work in a shorter period of time than you'd ever have imagined possible. You needn't do the challenge on just the bathroom—try any room in your house and set the timer for ten minutes. See how much you really can do in that small amount of time. Go ahead, challenge yourself!

When you're done, write down what you got done in ten minutes and how focused you managed to stay (using the Focus Meter technique). You'll quickly learn that the more focused you stay on

We All Love a Good Challenge!

Pretty much anyone loves a good challenge. Our competitive natures just seem to come to the fore when we're challenged to do something that seems impossible. If you tell your family or roommates to try to clean a room in under ten minutes, they'll balk and call you a cruel human being. If you make it all a bit of fun and challenge them to do it, you might have a very different scenario to deal with...including a tidier room! Just set the timer for ten minutes and choose one room for each participant. See who can get the most done in that amount of time. You could even offer prizes for the winners—hey, a reward or two is small payment indeed for help with the housecleaning!

that *one room*, the more you'll get done on a regular basis. I cannot stress how important this is, and trust me, it's a point I'm still working on myself (and probably always will be because I am by nature a curious and easily distracted sort). So take heart if you're the same, and just keep aiming for a 7 or 8 on the Focus Meter. For us, that's incredible!

Take Five

Even five minutes can equal a lot of cleaning done and finished in any room of your home. So you really don't have ten minutes to spare today to do some focus-room cleaning? Okay, I believe you. But do you have five minutes? I'll bet you could spare just five minutes. Once you get used to cleaning with a timer, you'll soon learn that a lot more is done by staying focused and on track than by wandering around the house in a willy-nilly way. (Okay, I admit, I really wanted to use that phrase somewhere in this book! How can you say willy-nilly and not giggle?)

Even tasks that seem laborious and lengthy can be done very quickly. Challenge yourself to vacuum any one room in your home in only five minutes. Or try tidying up any room for five minutes and see how much good it does. Sometimes our own perceptions of the

Stay focused and you'll accomplish more work than you ever imagined possible!

amount of time it takes to clean a room convince us not to even try, and therefore our homes just get messier and become less comfortable. Try these time challenges for yourself and prove to yourself how much you really can do in a limited amount of time. I know you can do it, and in fact I'm cheering you on!

YOUR FOCUS-ROOM CLEANING CHART

A Focus-Room Cleaning Chart will help you keep up with your focus-room cleaning. (See pages 197–203 for an example chart.) The chart sounds terribly organized and impressive, but it's just a listing of all the areas and rooms in your home. While I call it focus-*room* cleaning, this technique can in fact be used for specific problem areas that aren't separate rooms, such as a closet within a room or a dresser within a room. If it'll take at least ten minutes to work on it, and you can't get to it during cleaning bursts, it should be on your Focus-Room Cleaning Chart. Keep your Focus-Room Cleaning Chart on the fridge to make it easy to see at a glance what your schedule is (and so everyone else in the household can see it, too).

As already mentioned, you can accomplish a lot of cleaning when you do a focus-room cleaning. Just look at what you might be able to do in a ten-minute focus-room cleaning session:

- **Bathroom:** Scrub the tub and shower; scrub the toilet inside and out and sweep and mop the floor; declutter the medicine cabinet and under the sink; carefully clean the mirror.
- **Bedroom:** Vacuum and dust; straighten up the closet; clean out under the bed (ack! It's one of clutter's favorite hiding spots); straighten up dresser drawers.
- **Kitchen:** Wipe down the shelves in the refrigerator and toss any expired food; scrub the inside of the oven; mop the floor.

- *Living room:* Vacuum and dust; wash the windows; declutter end tables and recycle old newspapers and magazines.
- *Home office:* Vacuum and dust (don't forget the computer and keyboard); clean off your desk and clean off a bulletin board; declutter a bookshelf.
- *Storage area or garage:* Take one section per session and completely rearrange and declutter this area. Once it's organized, sweep on a regular basis and make sure the area stays tidy.
- *Kids' rooms:* Vacuum and dust; straighten up the closet; straighten up clothes in the dresser drawers; regularly sort clothes and toys for charity.

Persistent, Not Perfect

What if you can't do a focus-room cleaning every day? No worries! Aim for a few times every week, and build up if possible. Or just do a focus-room cleaning on days when you have time. You'll still see huge improvements over the long run. I can't stress enough that *No-Hassle Housecleaning* should make your life less stressful, not more stressful. So start with as many focus-room cleanings as you can and work from there. And remember that it's flexible—on slower weeks maybe you can get four days of focus-room cleaning done. On insane weeks packed with activities and appointments, two days with some focus-room cleaning is a major accomplishment. Use your Focus-Room Cleaning Chart so you can remember what room comes next, in case your pattern or routine is interrupted.

Focus-room cleaning is a great time for decluttering, washing, scrubbing—all those cleaning tasks you just can't get to in a short burst.

SCHEDULING YOUR FOCUS-ROOM CLEANING TIMES

Next you need to decide *when* you can do your daily focus-room cleaning. Everyone has a different lifestyle and schedule, so the time will be different for each one of us. Do the mornings work best for you? Or are evenings a better option? Would you prefer to do all your cleaning at once and just tackle the focus room right after your morning or evening cleaning burst? Decide on a specific time that will work best for you. If you find it doesn't work out, try another time until you've gotten a system of scheduling that works for you. And honestly, we all have days (sometimes lots of days) when we just don't have time to do our focus-room cleaning. On crazy days when life is coming at you two hundred miles a minute, don't worry! Knowing there will be days when you cannot possibly do a focus-room cleaning will assuage the guilt you might feel. *No-Hassle Housecleaning* means no worries, too! You'll always have tomorrow to handle that focus-room cleaning, so don't give it another worried thought.

6

Step Three: Weekly Clean-for-Alls

Cleaning bursts are fantastic, but they aren't terribly thorough. And focus-room cleaning is more thorough but still takes only ten minutes a day. More is still required for those occasional tasks or extra chores that pop up for all of us around our homes. This is where our weekly clean-for-all comes in. The clean-for-all finishes up some tasks you didn't get to during the week and is when you can handle other larger cleaning issues. And it's a fantastic time for the family to get more involved in your new cleaning routine!

The clean-for-all won't take as long as you might think. As you do your daily cleaning bursts and focus-room cleaning, your house will be a lot cleaner to begin with, so this weekly clean won't be all that hard. Put on some fantastic music to boogie to and get started!

You are doing so well! If you've already established the new habits of cleaning bursts and focus-room cleaning, I'm incredibly proud of you. I'm sure you're already seeing some terrific results, and your family and friends have probably noticed a big change, too. Isn't it amazing how utilizing a few tips and tricks can make such a huge difference in how comfortable your home really is?

Now that you're onto step three, the clean-for-all, I want to give you a hearty pat on the back for all the hard work you've done so far. Before you get down and dirty with the third step of your cleaning plan, you should know why the clean-for-all is an important step, not just a meaningless addition. With daily cleaning bursts and regular focus-room cleaning sessions, your home is already greatly improved. Now the clean-for-all is your chance to do some deeper cleaning you can't get to at any other time during the week. Because your home is already cleaner, you'll have fewer distractions and less prep before you can dig right in to some larger cleaning tasks. You can devote an entire clean-for-all to just one large cleaning job and get it done and over with. The 3-Step Solution wouldn't be complete without this all-important final step. You'll take your home from neat and tidy to clean and healthy.

Are You Ready for the Clean-for-Alls?

When you try to take on too many new habits at once, you're more likely to crash and burn—and all your good habits will end up in flames along with your original good intentions. To ensure this doesn't happen, make sure you start doing the last of the three steps—the clean-for-all—only after you've gotten completely used to doing your daily cleaning bursts and a number of focus-room cleaning sessions each week. Then, when those have become comfortable habits—like a pair of lovely, fuzzy slippers—you'll be ready to take on the last habit—the weekly clean-for-all.

CREATE A CLEAN-FOR-ALL PLAN

Your home needs its very own personalized clean-for-all plan. During your daily cleaning bursts and your focus-room cleaning, take note of areas that need more attention—areas you'd like to tackle during the clean-for-all. Remember to keep a notepad and pen in your cleaning kit so you don't have to go searching for these during your precious and brief cleaning-burst allotment. Over time, you'll have a rather lengthy list of additional tasks you'd like to tackle, ones you'll add to your clean-for-all list.

Budget Your Time

You're a hip and happy slob, so you have better things to do on the weekend than clean your beloved abode, right? But the weekend typically is the best time for the clean-for-all, because it's when most of us are off work, *and* it's when more visitors drop by. Having our homes looking and feeling comfortable and tidy is most important on these two days.

Your Notepad = Your Cleaning Lifeline

Your notepad really will become a lifeline to you when you're cleaning the happy slob's no-hassle way. Get into the habit of keeping a mini notepad with you during all your cleaning sessions (both cleaning bursts and focus-room cleanings) and jot down any trouble areas that will eventually need to be undertaken. This doesn't mean every item on the list will be handled that week. But you can strike off different tasks as you accomplish them, numbering them according to importance.

Before you begin, decide how much time you have to spend on the clean-for-all this week. Twenty minutes? Thirty? An hour or two? Whatever is realistic for you will work just fine, but between fifteen minutes and an hour is common.

The clean-for-all is your chance to do some deeper cleaning.

(Of course, this will also depend greatly on the size of your home.) Divvy up the clean-for-all tasks among everyone in the household and set your timer. On your mark, get set…go!

Work Smarter, Not Harder

Remember, the clean-for-all is different from focus-room cleaning, so you can focus on your entire house (that's why it's a clean-for all). If you plan to vacuum or mop all the floors in your house, budget your time so you'll get this arduous task over and done with in an efficient way. Make sure the floors in every room are clear and ready to be cleaned and then grab that broom and mop or vacuum and go to it. You can move from one room to the next without breaking your rhythm, and before you know it you'll be done. Have a plan of action that goes clearly in one direction—maybe the main floor first, then the next room, then the next, then stairs, then up to the second floor. The goal, of course, is to get as much essential cleaning done as possible—in one fell swoop! So instead of backtracking and wasting valuable time you could be using to do all sorts of other fabulous things, track out your plan of attack in one logical, circular motion.

Funky, Fresh Family Cleaning

If you have family members at home, you'll definitely want to get them in on the clean-for-all. As I've mentioned before, and maybe you've discovered for yourself, nagging really doesn't work. What does? Letting your family in on the plan of attack and creating a fun sort of competition work far better than nagging. And making the household cleaning fun and laid back will help tremendously, too—so don't get too fussy about their cleaning efforts. Everyone giving an honest effort matters more than perfect results. Remember, we happy slobs are so *not* about perfection!

Just get one or two larger tasks done and you've done a great job!

So get out your trusty timer and show your family that although your cleaning time will be limited, during this time you really want to see how much all of you can accomplish. Then set that timer, put on some music and get to it!

YOUR CLEAN-FOR-ALL PLAN OF ATTACK

Your clean-for-all should finish off a few things you couldn't complete during the week. Or it should involve larger cleaning and organizing tasks that need to be undertaken only occasionally. But don't think you'll be able to get everything done on your list every single week. At first you'll have tons of tasks lined up in your notebook.

Don't Backtrack, Jack!

Backtracking means retracing your steps, redoing what you think is a job not perfectly done. The problem with backtracking is that you also get off track with your overall plan of attack (try saying that ten times…). When vacuuming, dusting or mopping, work in one circular direction, and when you're done, you're done. Getting over the idea that cleaning must be perfect will be a major accomplishment and will give you greater peace of mind.

Just get one or two of those tasks done during your clean-for-all and you've done a great job! As time goes along, you'll notice that the overall length of that to-do list gets smaller and smaller as you get more and more things accomplished. Hurray!

Your clean-for-all is the best time for tasks such as a weekly fridge cleaning, mopping the floors in your home and larger-scale vacuuming. You can also do a deep clean on your bathrooms, if needed, or clean the oven. If you never seem to have time to dust during your focus-room cleaning, dust during your clean-for-all. Your house will look better, will smell fresher and you'll breathe easier. Look through what notes you jotted down in your notepad during the week and add any unfinished business to the clean-for-all. Get as much done as you can in your budgeted time. Stay focused on each task and finish it fully before going on to the next—this can be an incredibly difficult challenge if you're anything like me and are very easily distracted. Having your timer set will help to keep you focused on the tasks at hand.

SPRING CLEANING—EVEN IN WINTER

Depending on the type of home you have, there will be extra larger-scale cleaning and organizing tasks that simply cannot get accomplished during your cleaning bursts and focus-room cleaning sessions. Oftentimes these are called "spring cleaning" chores because after a long and drudging winter, we naturally want to tidy and spruce up our homes for the warmer weather that—thankfully—lies just ahead. But you needn't wait until springtime to perform all these tasks. Some can be undertaken even in the dark days of winter. Occasionally devote a clean-for-all session to some of these projects. So what are some of these larger-scale cleaning jobs that need to be undertaken once in a while?

- **Window washing:** A great task for the whole family to get involved in! Traditionally a "spring cleaning" chore that needs to be undertaken only once every year or so, window wash-

Funky Fridge Be Gone!

A nasty and neglected fridge can be a frightening proposition. Keep that appliance in good shape by clearing out old food and wiping down the inside and outside every week with your trusty Very Vinegar spray cleaner or any good all-purpose cleaner. It's a good time to replace a box of baking soda, if you keep one in your fridge like I do, to naturally absorb nasty, lingering odors (just once a month is fine). An especially good time to do this is before you do your weekly grocery shopping because you'll be able to put your new culinary delights into a lovely, clean refrigerator, which is so much more appealing than a science project gone wild!

ing is definitely
one to do in nice
weather—un-
less you want the
window-washing
water to freeze
into interesting
icicle-inspired
shapes on your
windows. (P.S.
the Very Vinegar
spray cleaner is fabulous on windows. That and a bunch of
newspapers will get those windows squeaky clean—your
grandmother probably washed her windows the same way.)

> Tackle larger "spring cleaning" tasks year-round during clean-for-alls.

- *Washing walls:* Every once in a while your walls need a good
  scrub down. Just a simple solution of a squirt of natural liquid
  soap in a bucketful of warm water will work well. To make it
  easier on yourself, try using a sponge mop to basically mop
  the walls clean. A little sprinkle of baking soda in the wash-
  ing-up liquid will add an extra blast of scrubbing power and
  naturally help neutralize odors. A two-in-one bonus!
- *Carpet (and upholstery) cleaning:* Manufacturers suggest
  cleaning your carpets once a year (or a little more often in
  high-traffic areas). You can rent a steam carpet cleaner at
  many locations, including supermarkets or home supply
  stores. Or you can purchase your own steam cleaner or go
  halvsies with a friend or family member to cut down on the
  initial outlay of funds. The same machine likely will have a
  special upholstery attachment that makes it easy to clean your

What if I Miss a Clean-for-All This Week?

I'm sure you know the answer to this question by now. Remember, the whole philosophy of *No-Hassle Housecleaning* is this: No more guilt! I know how insane life can get, so if you can't do a clean-for-all this week, you know what? That's okay. Life will go on, I promise you. Just try to do one as soon as you realistically can and as often as your life will allow. There, is that bad old guilt gone? Good, I love banishing nasty, old, grimy guilt. It seriously just wastes our time and energy.

upholstered furniture. Your sofa and cushy chairs will thank you for their marvelous makeover!

- **Closet decluttering:** This is a good time to get to work on decluttering an entire closet (or two...or three... You get the picture). Challenge your family members to declutter their closets—and offer rewards, such as a family dinner out if everyone works for twenty minutes on tidying their closets. Take old clothes no longer needed to charities; it's a valuable lesson for children to see the good their old clothes can do for people who really need them.

- **Cleaning light fixtures and ceiling fans:** These often-forgotten but ever-important items get pretty dusty over time, especially if the fan is used frequently. Use a long-handled duster or the upholstery attachment on your vacuum to clean these up. They'll look brand-new again.

- **Decluttering the pantry and kitchen cabinets:** Do you still have an old cake mix from the nineties lingering in the back of your pantry? Then you're a good candidate to do a pantry purge! Every six months or so, do a major pantry purge, getting rid of food items that are past due and vacuuming out the area to discourage little crawly critters from visiting. Do the same for your kitchen cabinets, clearing out old food, decluttering and wiping out the cabinets. Check storage containers to make sure they seal properly—another way to avoid uninvited guests into essentials such as flour and cereals.

7

The F-Word: Floors

No wonder our floors get so messy! With our stinky bare feet, pets' paws, wandering toddlers and everything we unceremoniously drag into our homes on the bottoms of our shoes and boots, our poor floors get quite a battering. That makes them difficult to clean—a challenge most happy slobs don't relish. First things first, you need three basic tools for floors: a good sturdy broom to sweep up the dirt, a decent mop and bucket to scrub and a vacuum or carpet sweeper for carpeted surfaces and rugs. Turn to page 45 for General Clean's Floor Cleaner, an easy, two-ingredient recipe for almost any type of floor.

Daily Floor Cleaning

Floors don't need to be cleaned daily unless you have a toddler waddling around who has an interest in eating off that floor. Every couple days is adequate to sweep, and once a week is adequate to mop. Mopping is also a great task for your clean-for-all because it can eat up a lot of time during your cleaning bursts.

SWEEP IT UP

You need only a broom and dustpan. Quick, sweeping motions get all the dust into the middle of the floor—that's where you want it. Then one big swoop, and you have it collected in the dustpan, ready to throw away. Some people bypass the broom and dustpan altogether and just use a vacuum on their hard floors. To use a vacuum cleaner on bare floors, just ensure that your vacuum has an adjustable setting especially intended for carpet-free surfaces, and switch the setting accordingly. Many modern vacuums have settings that run the full flooring gamut—from bare floors to thick-pile carpeting.

To take even less time to sweep, invest a few bucks in one of those new sweepers with attached throwaway cloths that use static electricity to keep the dirt stuck on. They eliminate the need for a dustpan altogether. Plus you can save yourself money by simply washing those cloths in soap and water and then air drying before reusing. Or invest in some reusable cloths easily ordered on the Internet that are more durable and intended to replace those throwaway cloths altogether. Easier on your pocketbook and the environment!

Sweeping is a great chore for kids and lazy roommates—get

To Sweep or Not to Sweep

While you technically don't need to sweep the floors every day, it's a great habit to get into with your evening cleaning burst! By sweeping the floors in the kitchen/dining area every day, you'll never have such an overwhelming crumby mess to deal with again. And this is a perfect task to get your kids involved in. Most little housecleaners like sweeping more than any other cleaning chore.

them involved. Throw a broom or sweeper into their hands and then turn on some funky music and ask them to show you their greatest dance moves—the only rule being that they must keep that broom on the floor at all times. In no time they'll be breathless *and* the floors will be swept. Free entertainment and a cleaner floor—it's all good!

MOP IT UP: CHOOSING THE BEST MOP

There are so many types of mops available on the market you can easily choose the one you like best to make mopping the floors an easier task than ever before. And remember to always thoroughly sweep first to remove any heavy surface dirt when you mop the floors so they'll be sparkling and streak-free.

1. *Traditional string mops:* Also called yacht mops or yarn mops, these are the classic mops with long strings we usually envision when we think of mops. This type requires a bucket or pail and some sort of wringing device to squeeze all the excess moisture from the mop. These are easy to use and cover a wide area of flooring in very little time, especially if you have a fairly large mop. Downside? They can be harder to clean and can get musty quickly. And it isn't always easy to replace the heads. Plus you always have to tote a bucket along with you.

A Happy Slob's Sweepy Trick

Do you hate it when dirt sticks to the broom bristles? Spray a bit of furniture polish on the bottom of the bristles, and dirt won't clump and stick anymore! It makes it easier to collect dirt, too.

2. **Sponge mops:** These simple mops are basically thick sponges on long handles. They usually come equipped with some sort of squeezer to remove excess moisture, are easy to use, and the sponges are usually quite easy to replace. You can dunk this into a bucket and then squeeze or just squirt a little floor cleaner directly on the floor as you go, foregoing the bucket altogether. (This technique is especially useful for quick cleaning jobs.)

3. **Sweeper mops with disposable refills:** A happy slob's greatest mopping buddy! Once you've swept the floor clean, a quick swipe with this sweeper mop will get the floor clean with very little effort. Then you can throw away the dirty pad. Or a more environmentally friendly option is to purchase a reusable microfiber pad to top these mops. Just rinse and pop the cloth into the washing machine. (I've discovered that clean, old dishcloths work just fine as replacement cloths.) You can use a sprayer bottle filled with Very Vinegar cleaner, or water with a tiny squirt of liquid dish soap, and spray and mop!

4. **Microfiber mops:** These popular new mops use incredible microfiber material to clean the floors. They are usually easy to maneuver as they have flat heads that can be replaced. The plus side of cleaning with microfiber is that you don't have to use any additional cleaners—just water. So just rinse the mop head occasionally with water and keep on cleaning!

To sum up the mystery of the mops, I like the sweeper mops with refills for regular use. They're so easy to use! And you can easily forego the refill cloths by using microfiber cloths or even old dishcloths.

VA-VA-VOOM VACUUMING

Yes, vacuuming really can be exciting enough to earn this quirky title! If you don't have a vacuum, borrow one *or* purchase an inexpensive carpet sweeper. If you're fortunate enough to have all hard floors, you really don't need a vacuum at all. Most of us have at least some carpet or a few rugs to deal with, though, so a vacuum is a necessity.

I've heard people say there's a "correct" way to vacuum, which is to do it in a neat pattern so all the vacuum marks go in one direction. Okay, all together: Let's roll our eyes at this concept. Only professional cleaners with fussy, rich clients need to be so precise. (And even then, don't they have more to worry about than carpet patterns?) The dirt and dust don't care what direction you go in! If you have only a few minutes to spare, do a quick vacuum job—it makes a huge difference. It'll look great, even if the pattern on the floor looks like an unsolvable jigsaw puzzle by the time you're done.

Then, when you have more time, attach the hose attachment and get into the nooks and crannies and the edges of the floor. This needs doing only occasionally—maybe once a month or so.

TLC FOR FLOOR TYPES

Different floors need different care. Here are some no-hassle cleaning tips for all the floors in your home:

- *Wood:* According to the Wood Flooring Manufacturers Association, wood and water simply don't mix. If your wood floors are treated with polyurethane finish, you can use water sparingly—such as a slightly dampened cloth or mop with a splash of white vinegar for cleaning power. If, on the other hand, your wood floors are treated with a wax finish, *never*

Suck it Up: Vacuuming Tips

- *Sprinkle plain baking soda* on carpets before vacuuming and let it sit for about ten to fifteen minutes; it will naturally absorb stinky odors from deep inside the carpet pile, and after you vacuum the carpet will smell fresh and clean—naturally. This is an excellent replacement for those store-bought carpet fresheners.

- *Another baking-soda vacuum tip:* Sprinkle a bit right in the vacuum bag or waste container every time you empty it. It helps keep musty odors to a minimum within the vacuum.

- *Before buying a new vacuum cleaner,* do your research. There are many consumer review Web sites on which people share their firsthand opinions of products. These are excellent places to check before heading out to purchase your new vacuum cleaner because you'll learn which ones work well in real-life situations. The best vacuum cleaner likely won't be the cheapest one, but in the long run you'll save money by not having to replace it quickly. (On the other hand, the priciest model isn't always the best either.) Also make sure the vacuum is light enough for everyone in the family to use, including junior happy slobs. Heavy vacuums make the chore twice as hard as it needs to be.

- *If anyone in your family has allergies,* a Hepa filter in your new vacuum is a must. It effectively filters out the majority of allergens and dust—a big plus for allergy sufferers.

use water at all on your floors. It can leave spots and splotches and can dull the finish. Instead, look for specialty wood-floor cleaners meant for use on the finish your floors have. Check with your manufacturer to see what's best for your floors. You also can *test* to see if your floor has a wax or polyurethane finish—drop a single droplet of water onto an inconspicuous area. If, after evaporating, it leaves a small white circle, you have a waxed finish. Use a little floor wax to remove the spot, and then be sure to contact the manufacturer for a recommended cleaner. If your floor doesn't show that telltale white spot, your floors are likely finished in polyurethane, and you can safely use a white vinegar/water solution.

- *Linoleum or vinyl floors:* These are a happy slob's best flooring friend! They're simple to care for—just a small squirt of liquid soap in a bucketful of water is all it takes, and then mop away. Use only a little soap, or it can leave a sticky residue that actually attracts dirt, making it harder to clean over time. You can also use club soda in a spray bottle to clean your floors without taking out a bucket! Just give it a good spray and use a moistened mop to clean the floors. And of course there are a host of commercial mopping products to choose from if you prefer that route.

- *Carpets:* Shampooing carpets once or twice a year helps your carpets retain a newer, fresher look. It's also more sanitary as it removes stains and soil from deep within the carpet fibers. You can rent a carpet cleaner from most grocery and hardware stores, or you can purchase one or share it with friends and family to split the cost. Quickly blotting up spills when they happen will make it easier to keep your carpet looking great.

- **Ceramic tiles:** A solution of ½ cup of white vinegar in a bucket of clean water can be used to clean these beautiful floors. Never use soap on ceramic tile floors, as it can dull the finish.
- **Marble:** Wow, you're a posh happy slob, aren't you, what with your swanky marble floors? That's okay, we still love you, and here's how to clean those floors: Again, white vinegar comes heroically to the rescue! About a half cup in your cleaning bucket, filled the rest of the way with clean tap water, will do the job nicely. In European countries, where marble floors are more common, they'll even substitute a cup of white wine instead of the white vinegar. Sounds good to me. Or else you could just sip that nice glass of wine between cleaning bursts. Sounds even better!

8
You're Surrounded! Cleaning Walls and Windows

You might have heard the common lament of housecleaners: "We don't do windows." Window cleaning (along with wall cleaning) is the chore not even professional cleaners like to do. So how is a happy slob to conquer these windows and walls that surround us? Easy! Just a few tips and techniques will turn these dreaded tasks into something easier and less stressful. And remember that these cleaning chores need to be undertaken only occasionally, so take heart.

WACKY WALL-CLEANING SOLUTION AND TECHNIQUE

This solution is wacky because it uses ingredients that are off the wall (hardy-har-har), yet it works to remove the grime, grit, marks and fingerprints that collect on our walls over time. See the recipe at the bottom of page 93. Having a friend or family member help with this chore will reduce the time involved as the cleaning solution does need to be rinsed off after it's applied.

As always, put on some funky music to make this chore more fun. And if you want to avoid this chore altogether, do as one clever lady at the paint counter once told me: "If you don't want to wash the walls, just paint them!" (More on painted walls later on in this chapter.)

> *Just a few techniques will turn these dreaded tasks into something easier.*

Dip the mop into the solution and then squeeze out the excess. Use the mop to reach all areas of the wall without a ladder. I'm not a big fan of ladders (slight fear of heights) so I do whatever I can to avoid them and not cause bodily harm to myself.

Wacky Wall-Cleaning Solution

> 1 cup borax (found in the laundry section of any grocery store)
> 3 tbsp. baking soda
> 3 tbsp. liquid dish soap
> Bucket of warm water
> Sponge mop

Combine all ingredients in a big pail of warm water and use a clean sponge mop to swish it all around until the water is a bit sudsy and the borax and baking powder are dissolved. (Important note: Test a small, inconspicuous area first to make sure this cleaner won't damage your wall's finish.)

Once done, rinse out the mop and fill the bucket with clean water. Use the mop and clean water to rinse off the areas already cleaned. *Or* convince a dear friend to follow behind you with a clean bucket of water and another sponge mop, rinsing as you finish the cleaning. It's much easier that way. Your walls will shine! And you'll bond with your buddy over the cleaning.

While you're at it, you'll want to pay a little attention to those often ignored but oh-so-useful doors! Doors can easily get mucky, especially if you have pets or children. Wipe down doors with the wall-cleaning solution or a simple solution of a small squirt of dish-washing soap in a bucket of warm water. You don't need the mix to be too soapy—just enough to clean but not enough to be sticky and actually attract more dirt. Wipe clean with a damp sponge dipped in fresh water to rinse off any lingering soap residue.

HOW OFTEN SHOULD I CLEAN MY WALLS?

Whenever they get mucky. I realize that's not a terribly specific answer, but it really does depend on how dirty your walls get. A good cleaning two times a year should suffice in the kitchen, unless your family has a habit of throwing their spaghetti and spaghetti sauce on the wall to test before chowing down on delicious Italian feasts. In which case, you'll need to scrub those walls far more often. And check into getting a brand-new, cleverer family while you're at it.

Only the kitchen walls need such frequent cleaning. The other walls in your home will require a wipe-down only once a year or even less often. The paint color on your walls also helps determine how often you'll need to clean them—cream and taupe shades and other darker colors don't show the grime as quickly as bright white walls. So happy slobs will definitely want to look into painting their

Dirty, Dirty Doorknobs

Want to know something sort of gross? The doorknobs in your home can harbor more germs and bacteria than the toilet seats! I know, it's an icky thought, but one that should remind you to wipe down your doorknobs when you're cleaning in any particular room. A quick swipe with a natural disinfectant cleaner will kill those nasty little critters. Do this more often when someone in the household has a cold or the flu to prevent the further spread of germs.

Doorknobs are cleaned in different ways according to what type of doorknob you have. Cheapo doorknobs (like I have!) are easily cleaned with a disinfectant cleaner to kill all the germs that like to linger there. But if you have classic brass doorknobs, treat them to a little loving care once in a while by shining them up with some brass cleaner. You can find brass cleaner at most hardware stores, or try making it yourself. Mix together ½ cup white vinegar with 1 tablespoon table salt. The acid and salt work together to clean up dingy brass doorknobs, leaving them looking good as new. Polish up afterward with a lint-free, soft cloth. And, as we happy slobs love, there are no harmful chemicals involved.

walls with fresh and bright colors—for the creative aspect *and* to hide dirt sufficiently!

CHOOSING A PAINT FINISH

That funny lady at the paint counter might have had a legitimate point—instead of cleaning your walls, you can simply slop on a fresh coat of paint. If you're in the market for new paint, you'll want to consider more than just the fashionable color. Different types of

Removing Crayon Marks from Walls

It's the bane of every parent—those dreaded colorful smudges your little artiste has decided to bless the wall with. First, try dipping a damp cleaning cloth into a little baking soda and rubbing away the spot. If that doesn't work, get out the heavy artillery! Crayon marks can be removed with a sponge and some WD-40 (a brand of lubricant/cleaner available in most hardware stores). Just add a little to the sponge and work in a circular motion on the stain and repeat if necessary. Always be sure to test in an inconspicuous area first to make sure your wall finish can handle this cleaning without being damaged.

paint finishes will make it either easier or harder to clean your walls later on. Here's a little debriefing on paint types:

- *Flat:* This paint type is entirely without gloss and is good for areas with very low traffic because flat paint is almost impossible to clean. That does, however, make it a good choice for ceilings. It's good to keep a little extra of this paint on hand because if you do get marks on the surface, it's easier to touch up than to clean.

- *Eggshell:* Eggshell finish is an ideal name for this paint because if you imagine the look of an eggshell—mostly matte with the tiniest bit of sheen—you can envision how this paint will look on your walls. It's slightly easier to clean than flat paint and a very popular choice overall.

- *Semigloss:* This paint provides some true cleanability and is especially good to use in areas like kids' rooms, where you'll want to be able to scrub the walls over and over again.

But prepare the walls carefully before painting, as this level of gloss paint will highlight imperfections far more than a matte finish.

- **Gloss:** Gloss paint is really easy to clean, but the highly glossy look isn't suitable for covering walls. And gloss paint will show any and all imperfections in the wall or surface. Because I'm sure you don't want super shiny walls, this paint is better kept for painting funky accessories or your front door.

Ask your local paint supplier for tips on new varieties of paint that are easier to clean, or ask which types of paint you should use in which areas of your home.

CLEANING WALLPAPER OR PANELING

If your walls aren't painted but are papered or paneled, you'll need a few unique tips to aid in your cleaning. Wallpaper is making a comeback as a fashionable way to add a splash of color or pattern to an otherwise boring wall. And, thankfully, many varieties are easy to clean, especially the types with a thin vinyl coating. To clean, good old soap and water and a sponge should do the trick—make sure to avoid any harsh cleaners that could damage the wallpaper. The only type of wallpaper that is difficult to clean is the paper that has no vinyl coating to protect the surface. When in doubt, always contact the wallpaper manufacturer to check on specific cleaning instructions for their product.

Wood paneling is coated with a protective finish, which helps make cleaning far easier. Just one small squirt of mild dishwashing liquid in a bucketful of water is all you need. First, dust off the surface with a duster or clean cloth and then use a sponge dipped into the water to wipe the surface clean and remove any soapy residue. If your wood paneling needs a deeper cleaning, old-fashioned oil soap is a good option. Follow the instructions on the bottle.

LOOKING OUT AT THE WORLD: WINDOWS AND WINDOW COVERINGS

No, I'm not talking about your computer's operating system. These windows are the ones that bring the beauty of the outdoors right into our own living areas.

This is an occasional chore you might want to get help with because it is a bit of a bother for most of us happy slobs. You can bribe your friends with homemade cookies, delivery pizza and cheap beer—whatever works for them. Clean windows only once (or twice) a year. You won't have to pay your friends for their cheap labor often.

WINDOWS CLEANING

When tackling window cleaning, you'll want to first clean the window frames, which can gather dust—especially in warm weather when we love leaving the windows open. Often made of painted

✳ While You're at It

There's more than paint on them there walls, cowboy. Yes, there are lovely pictures, mirrors and shelves to contend with, too. While you're working on the walls, don't forget to give the mirrors and pictures a dust and shine with a duster, cloth and shiny cleaner as you go. Your walls will look great! And so will all the decorative doodads on them.

aluminum, window frames need to be cleaned very gently—as anything too harsh or abrasive can damage the painted surface. Just a bit of soapy water will do the trick with a bit of gentle scrubbing action provided by the same damp cloth dipped into baking soda. (Be careful though because the painted surface really can be quite delicate.)

For small-scale cleaning jobs, use our homemade Window and Glass Cleaner recipe in Chapter 3 or any commercial glass cleaner. Use newspapers to wipe rather than paper towels, as paper towels leave behind nasty streaks and lint.

A squeegee costs only a few dollars and is a marvelously helpful little tool for large or small cleaning jobs because it wipes the windows clean, clear and streak-free. Spray on some cleaner and use your regular sponge to scrub the window. Then use the squeegee to wipe off the surface. Wipe off the squeegee blade with a paper towel before working on the next section of window. If you don't have a squeegee, just spray on some cleaner and use scrunched-up newspaper to scrub the windows clean.

For exterior window cleaning, consider using one of the new types of window cleaners that attach right to your garden hose. The cleaner comes in an attachment that screws on to the hose nozzle, and then when the water sprays out of the hose, it contains a mixture of cleaner. The water pressure plus the cleaner make cleaning windows an absolute breeze!

More Window-Washing Tips

- *Screened out: Washing screens.* Scrub outdoor screens with soapy water, rinse them and then allow them to dry. Other screens can be vacuumed with the upholstery attachment to remove dirt and dust.

- *Make mine a microfiber cloth.* Because they don't leave lint behind, microfiber cloths are very handy to have around when cleaning windows. Some are made especially for cleaning glass and mirrors, and you don't even need to use any chemicals with them—just water. What a great way to protect your health and the environment!
- *Cloudy-day window-cleaning foray.* Wash your windows on a cloudy day. If the sun is too bright and intense, your windows will dry too quickly and be streaky.

Whatever method of window cleaning you choose, you can now let the sun shine in because your windows are looking fantastic. Bravo! That wasn't such a horrible task now, was it?

CLEANING BLINDS

When you wash the windows, don't forget the blinds and curtains around them. While you *can* buy a pricey blind-cleaning gadget if you really want to, I think an altogether better way is to use a clean paintbrush. Or, for about five bucks or less, you can find a special little sponge cleaner with notches that make dusting blinds simple and quick. (Check your hardware store for these cleaning gizmos.) Or use the upholstery attachment from your vacuum cleaner to dust your blinds.

To clean plastic blinds thoroughly, you can remove them, hose them down outside and let them air dry before returning them to the house. Depending on how grimy your blinds get, once every year or two is as often as you'll need, perhaps only dusting them every few months to prevent a huge accumulation of dirt.

CLEANING CURTAINS

I think the ultimate solutions to cleaning curtains are wipe-down plastic curtains! Can't you imagine the benefits of just cleaning curtains with a sponge? Okay, if that's really not an option, and if you have regular fabric curtains, you will need to wash them once in a while. Stick with unfussy fabrics you can throw in the washing machine, or you'll likely need to haul them off to the dry cleaner's. *Or* use the special upholstery attachment on your vacuum cleaner to remove dust from curtains or blinds without having to take them down at all.

9

Do-Little Dusting

Dust is the bane of all happy slobs. Why? Because it's a never-ending cycle of dirt that collects in the most annoying places. Sometimes it feels like dusting is truly never done. Well, leave those negative thoughts behind because dusting is in fact one of the easiest housecleaning jobs around! (It's also another great task for kids, as long as you don't have a collection of rare china or crystal goblets on display. Few happy slobs do, by the way. We tend toward paper plates to make cleanup easier.)

WHAT YOU NEED
- A static-electric duster or microfiber duster (or a feather duster, if that's what you have or prefer)
- A few lint-free cloths or my new favorite, microfiber dusting cloths
- Wood polish (homemade or commercial—your choice)

Static-electric dusters are amazing because they do most of the dusting work for you. No, I'm not a duster manufacturer out to make huge sales with my propaganda—I'm just telling it like it is. I want to decrease your cleaning time as much as possible, and these things work! They're huge, fluffy monstrosities that look as silly as they are effective. Most department stores or hardware stores carry them, and I think they're twice as good as regular feather dusters. Anything that holds on to the dust for you is a good thing, if you ask me.

You'll also need to keep around a supply of dusting rags and wood polish if you have wooden surfaces to clean. You don't need to pull out the polish every time you dust, but definitely do it at least once a month to give Grandma's antique table a good shine and show it you still care. Polishing helps cut through the buildup that regular dry dusting doesn't accomplish.

By keeping a duster, cloths and polish in your regular cleaning kit,

Microfiber Dusters Do More!

Microfiber dusters and dusting cloths are the newest trend in home dusting. But they're more than just a clever marketing ploy—those little microfibers in each cloth are scientifically impressive. These fibers clutch on to dust molecules instead of just pushing them around. Thus, your dusting time is decreased, and the whole job becomes a lot simpler. You can choose from microfiber dusting cloths or new, fluffy microfiber dusters that have removable heads and can be popped into the washing machine for occasional cleaning. Find these in any good department store or in specialty retailers like kitchen shops. (You can also order microfiber cleaning cloths and dusters online—and often at a substantial savings.)

dusting is a breeze to accomplish anytime. Just swipe at the surface with the duster—this is where the static type really helps because it attracts dust. Once you're done dusting, give the duster a good shake outside. Remember always to dust first and then polish, or you're just moving the dust around in clumps of polish, which is not terribly effective.

WHY DUSTING MATTERS

So if dusting is a never-ending job with few rewards, why bother dusting in the first place? I have an answer for you that will get you hunting for a dusting cloth or feather duster, and I do mean now. Dust can be hard on our health—inhaling dust can aggravate allergies and asthma. So dusting isn't all about making your home look good, it's also a health issue.

Within that layer of innocent-looking dust are the little critters that feed on the dust—dust mites. These creatures feed on what dust is made of: dried skin, pet dander, mold spores, bits of food and other environmental stuff. Most of our allergies are due to the mites' waste, not the little creeps themselves. So dealing with dust means you get rid of these mites and their waste in one fell swoop. Dusting regularly and effectively can help reduce allergic reactions or asthma attacks. (Speak to your

Dusting is, in fact, one of the easiest housecleaning jobs around.

doctor or allergist if you're concerned about dust mites and other allergens in your home.)

Now that you have a little extra (thoroughly disgusting) motivation to get dusting, let's destroy that dust once and for all...or at least until the next dusting session comes around.

> *Always dust first and then polish. Otherwise, you are just moving dust around.*

DUSTING TIPS

- Silk flowers and plants are easier to clean when you put them in a paper bag with a few tablespoons of salt, close that bag and shake, shake, shake the dust right off them!
- If you're allergy-prone and plan to do a lot of dusting, wear a face mask. Yes, it'll look silly, but it'll help protect you from an attack of sneezing later on.
- TV screens and computer monitors are easy to dust when you use fabric-softener sheets—another fun, kid-friendly cleaning task, even for very little ones. Just toss sheets in the trash when finished. No fuss, no muss, and they will leave a streak-free, dusted shine. (You can also use fabric-softener sheets that have already been used in the drier; they'll still work fine.)
- Dusting ceiling fans can be an especially awkward chore; using the dusting attachment of your vacuum cleaner really helps make it easier. I've also discovered that you can purchase

specialty attachments for the vacuum just for cleaning ceiling fans. Check them out at a local vacuum-cleaner retailer or by searching online. If you have a lot of ceiling fans in your home, it might be worth the investment.

- Kids will have great fun dusting when you pop clean socks or mittens on their hands as their tools of choice. They can run their hands all around the surfaces and get them good and clean but still have fun.

- Feather dusters come in many varieties with long wand handles that adjust or extend to reach even the most awkward, tall areas of your home. Instead of reaching for a ladder or footstool, reach for one of these instead and make your dusting tasks easier and less terrifying, to boot!

- Start at the top when you dust and work down. As the dust falls down, you'll get it all swept away by the time you reach the bottom.

- Cleaning cobwebs is easier when you simply vacuum the mess away, using telescopic attachments that reach up high. Otherwise, grab a long broom and sweep the ceilings clean.

- A slightly dampened microfiber cleaning cloth is a great dusting option because it leaves no lint, and you can clean without any added chemicals. Slightly moistening it with water will make the dust stick easily.

- Soft, clean paintbrushes are excellent tools for dusting pleated lampshades and other nitpicky areas. Or try using your hair drier on the no-heat setting to blow away the dust.

- Reduce clutter to make dusting an easier chore. Fewer knick-knacks equal fewer surfaces for dust to collect on and therefore less dusting to do.

- If dusting makes you cough or sneeze, don a face mask or even a bandana around your nose and mouth when doing this chore. The mask will help prevent these reactions, and you'll look mysterious at the same time.

Sure, dusting may seem like a dreary job, but with these few tips you'll be on the road to becoming a duster extraordinaire! With these dusting essentials toted in your cleaning kit, you'll be able to dust that nasty stuff away.

10

Cleaning du Jour: The Kitchen

No wonder the kitchen is called the heart of a home—it's the spot where the cooking, eating, laughing, visiting and family conferences just naturally seem to occur! But all that fun and culinary experimentation can create quite a lot of havoc—and muck—along the way. Grease, grime and clutter seem to just spontaneously appear in this room, from mucky floors all the way up to sticky appliances and grungy cupboards. Argh! It's okay, we've got a handle on this situation. All you need is some information, and soon your kitchen will be more comfortable and appealing than ever before. Ready, set, clean!

CODE-RED CLEANING IN...THE KITCHEN!

Company's coming, and you're not exactly thrilled! They love clustering in the kitchen for chats and snacks, but the kitchen looks like a Tasmanian devil just strolled through. What to do? Get your family in on the cleaning action right this minute! Split up the following tasks among all of you.

1. Deal with dirty dishes, pronto. Nothing looks worse than a pile of nasty dishes all over the place. Clean out the dishwasher, quickly fill it again and start it. If you don't have a dishwasher, get your family to wash the dishes. If there are leftover pots and pans to clean, tuck them away in the stove to hide them. Just don't forget about them and leave them in there for a week! Yuck.

2. Do a fast sweep if the floors need it. If there are any mucky bits, use your all-purpose cleaner and a rag to clean those particular spots quickly instead of pulling out the mop and bucket. This is probably *not* the time to use your vinegar cleaner, as the scent won't be gone quickly enough.

3. Using your all-purpose cleaner, quickly wipe down the most visible areas in your kitchen, such as the stove, counters, etc. Don't have any cleaner? Just squirt a bit of liquid dish soap into a spray bottle, fill with water and now you do.

4. Turn the lights down—or light scented candles for ambience. Visitors won't see the excess mess!

5. Do a quick cleaning burst right in the kitchen. Get rid of clutter by throwing it in a plastic bag and putting it away in a closet until you can deal with it later.

6. Put on some coffee and relax—your kitchen will look fine. And if caffeine addicts are coming over, they'll notice only the coffee brewing anyway.

TOP, MIDDLE AND BOTTOM CLEANING

Although this sounds like a cheesy line from a workout video, this section's title helps us remember to clean more thoroughly. When we live in a home long enough, we stop really seeing the mess and clutter. Why? Because we're so darned used to seeing it every day it becomes invisible to us, just another part of the scenery. So take a walk into your kitchen as if you're seeing it for the first time. Try to see it for what it really is, not just what you've grown accustomed to.

Top: Starting at the top, you'll notice that a lot of clutter can find its way onto the tops of your surfaces—such as the tops of kitchen cabinets and appliances like microwaves and refrigerators. For those of us not blessed with great height, we might need a stepladder to see up there.

Middle: This is where the majority of cleaning is done because this is where all the cabinetry and appliances are found. During code-red cleaning sessions, you should focus on these areas because these are the spots your visitors will see the most.

Bottom: Cleaning kitchen floors can be a particularly challenging task for us happy slobs. A cup of white vinegar diluted in a bucketful of water is an excellent all-purpose kitchen floor cleaner. It kills germs and mold but doesn't harm you or the environment. See Chapter 7 for complete instructions on cleaning all types of floors.

DISHES

Some of my most creative childhood memories are of my cousin and me developing excuses to get out of washing dishes after family gatherings. She had the whole thing down to an art—she would develop horrible cramps and be stuck in the washroom (with her favorite book conveniently in hand) for an hour or more. Only after the rest of us had completed the job would she finally return to the land of the living.

I still am not a huge dishwashing fan, but I can't use my cousin's clever techniques. So let's face the monster together and just get the job done. Truth be told, dishwashing is an unpleasant problem in many households.

Whether you're a large family, a retired couple or roomies sharing a place, dishes may seem like an insurmountable enemy. Unless you eat out for every meal, you have to deal with dishes. Here, then, are nine ways to beat the dishwashing beast.

Nine Ways to Beat the Dishwashing Beast

1. **Reduce the dishes!** I don't mean to literally throw them away, but I do mean reduce how many you use. Warning roomies or family that they'll have to wash up the extra dirty dishes they create should help your conservation efforts.

2. **Let the dishwasher do the work.** If you have a dishwasher, use liquid dishwasher detergent for cleaner dishes. Instead of pricey rinse agents to achieve sparkling dishes, substitute white vinegar. Let the dishwasher run overnight and then you'll be ready to unload it in the morning. Plus, energy rates are cheaper at night.

3. **Make it a morning ritual.** Again, load your dishwasher and let it run during the night. Putting away the dishes should be part of your morning cleaning burst every day. If you handwash your dishes but let them air dry, you can still put away the dishes in the morning. It takes only a few minutes, and you can do it while you're putting the kettle on for coffee or tea. By the time your drink is ready, your dishes will be put away, too.

4. **Keep the sink empty.** When the dishwasher is done, empty it immediately so newly dirtied dishes can be put right into the dishwasher rather than gather in the sink. Clean the

sink with a shiny cleaner and then leave a warning note in the bottom: LEAVE DISHES HERE AND DIE. Maybe that's a tad too drastic, but you could leave a note that says dishes belong in the dishwasher, not the sink. Who would dare defy you?

5. *Wash dishes after each meal.* If you don't have a dishwasher, make an even more determined effort to reduce the number of dishes you use. Get into the habit of cleaning dishes right after you've dirtied them, so you don't get into that awful habit of letting them pile up like a bad art display. Buy sponges attached to handles that hold dish soap—they make washing dishes quick and easy. Instead of filling the sink with water, simply rinse your dish, scrub it with the sponge (the soap is released as you scrub) and rinse off the soap. You can wash plates and cups in seconds.

6. *Let it dry au naturel.* If you use hot water when handwashing, air drying will not leave streaks or spots, and it saves you tons of time. For the dishwasher, it helps reduce electricity costs.

7. *Try soaking, not scrubbing.* A little overeager when baking that lasagna? Nasty, baked-on gunk can be removed with a fabric-softener sheet! Add a sheet, fill the pan with water and let it sit overnight. In the morning it should clean up easily. (Note: Use this trick only on stainless or glass baking dishes. The fabric-softener sheet might actually damage or even remove nonstick surface treatments, so don't use it on any nonstick surface.)

8. *Teach others how take care of their own dishes.* Teach kids, roomies and all family members to clean up their own

dishes when they're done with them. After a drink of milk or a bowl of cereal, it takes only seconds to swipe the dish clean with a cloth and let it dry or to put it in the dishwasher. Commend them when they implement these new habits.

9. **Use paper plates.** Seriously! If dishes are a huge obstacle in your home, why not? Use recyclable ones so you won't have a guilty conscience.

CLEANING APPLIANCES

From sticky refrigerator doors to oven interiors that look positively unearthly, we know cleaning appliances is a tough job. It doesn't help that we usually procrastinate until the situation is completely out of hand. Here are ways to cut down on the amount of time you spend cleaning your appliances and yet still get them sparkling clean.

A general rule of thumb is that baking soda is your best friend when cleaning appliances. A bit sprinkled onto a wet cloth works better than anything to clean appliances without leaving nasty scratches, and of course it's chemical free, so you can breathe easy. Just give it a scrub with your soda-sprinkled cloth and then wipe off the soda with a moistened cloth. Sparkly!

Any all-purpose cleaning spray recipe from Chapter 3 will work safely on appliances. Again, a diluted white vinegar mixture

Baking soda is your best friend when cleaning appliances.

works great. Don't worry about the smell—it really does dissipate quickly. Trust me, and just try it. One of my favorite appliance cleaners is club soda. A bit in a spray bottle works great on any appliance, especially stainless steel, because it adds a lot of impressive shine. It doesn't matter a bit whether it's fresh or stale club soda, so it's a good way to use up that old stuff in the back of the fridge.

Refrigerator

The nastiest appliance cleaning job around! With spills and splatters inside and out, this one is a challenge even for neat freaks. So what hope is there for happy slobs? Here's the way to do the job right.

1. Prepare a bucket of warm, soapy water with a cloth and scrubby sponge soaking inside. Add a splash of white vinegar or baking soda to the water.
2. Empty the fridge completely. Throw away disgusting, unrecognizable leftovers.
3. Work from the top of the fridge down; as drips go to the bottom, you'll deal with them as you go.
4. Use the scrubby sponge to deal with gunky messes. A bit of baking soda will help scrub them away. If it's a stubborn bit of goo, pour a bit of baking soda right onto it, add a little

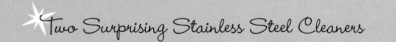

Two Surprising Stainless Steel Cleaners

For shining stainless steel surfaces, try two unlikely suspects: olive oil or rubbing alcohol. A bit of olive oil on a lint-free cloth will remove fingerprints and smudges, while the rubbing alcohol will finish things up with a streak-free shine.

water to make a paste, and let it sit for a few minutes while you finish the rest of the fridge. When you come back it should be easier to remove.

5. Once washed, wipe the inside dry with a clean cloth or paper towel.

6. Clean the outside with any all-purpose or shiny cleaner and a few cleaning rags.

Garbage Disposals

Stinky disposal got you down? Tackle the foul odors with a hearty sprinkle of baking soda (about ¼ to ½ cup) down the drain and then let it sit for a good half hour. Flush with boiling water. You can also try throwing down a sliced whole orange or lemon and a few cups of ice; all the lovely natural essential oils from the citrus rinds will grind up and make things smell lovely. The ice helps resharpen the disposal blades.

Stovetop and Oven

The stovetop and oven are other nasty kitchen cleaning tasks to tackle, but you can do it! The outside of the stove isn't so bad; an all-purpose cleaner or a bit of baking soda on a moistened rag or sponge works just fine. Clean drip trays by filling your sink about one-quarter full with water. Add a couple cups of white vinegar to the mix and let the drip trays soak at least an hour. The mess should wipe off easily.

Citrus fruits like lemons, limes and oranges are nature's own degreasing superheroes, so if you've got a greasy mess, grab a lemon or two from the fridge and work through grease with ease. The duo you'll want to try is lemon juice (fresh or bottled will work fine) and some baking soda. They work well together because the lemon juice cuts through grease naturally, while the baking soda adds serious scouring action.

The method to try: Sprinkle a little salt or baking soda on tough spots and then drizzle on some lemon juice. Let it sit for a few minutes—the baking soda and lemon juice will fizz up a bit—and then use either a sponge or the cut lemon itself to scour away the grease. Wipe clean with a cloth or paper towel. The stove will also smell nice and fresh now, reminiscent of lemonade in the summertime. Yum! We'll take that over toxins any day.

Cleaning the inside of the oven is the trickiest part, but again, white vinegar comes to the rescue. (I'm beginning to feel like the reigning Ms. Vinegar Advocate.) A strong white vinegar-water mixture (half white vinegar and half water) with a squirt of natural dishwashing liquid does the trick. Spray liberally inside the oven, close the oven door and let sit for an hour or two. Then get to cleaning with a moistened scrubby sponge.

Prevent nasty oven stains by cleaning spills quickly, not letting them dry into nasty masses of burned food. Just a little baking soda or even a bit of soap and water and a scrubby sponge help clean up fresh stains inside your oven.

Dishwashers

Dishwashers will need occasional cleaning both inside and out. The outside is simply a matter of using soapy water (or baking soda again) and a soft cloth.

The inside needs a little more attention. Pour a cup of white vinegar into the bottom and run an empty load. The white vinegar helps to clean the inside of the dishwasher.

Microwaves

Microwaves get really messy. Here's my favorite way to deal with the gunk: Take a regular household sponge and soak up a lot of water in it. Squirt a bit of lemon juice or white vinegar right onto the sponge. Plop it down in the middle of the messy microwave and heat for a minute or two. Now *let it sit* without opening the microwave door for at least fifteen minutes. All that beautiful steam will degunk and defunk your microwave with absolutely no effort on your part. Lovely, isn't it? It's doing all the work for you while you carry on and do other things.

After you've let the mixture sit in there and work its steamy magic, use that same sponge to simply wipe the mess away. Voilà, sparkling clean microwave. Now to add some sparkle to the lackluster exterior of the microwave. Try a good shiny cleaner (either made or purchased). Spray and then wipe it down to get it super shiny. Wouldn't your mom be proud?

Small Appliances

Coffeemakers are a breeze to clean. Just use your all-purpose cleaner or shiny cleaner with a soft cloth to clean the outside. To clean the inner workings of the machine itself, run white vinegar through instead of water and turn on the machine as normal. Pour out the vinegar and let the coffeemaker run through with cold, fresh water for two cycles after that to rinse out every last bit of vinegar. It really cleans out all the buildup, and your coffee will taste better than ever.

Toasters need to be shaken out once in a while, and you'll be entertained by the shower of crumbs! Wipe that away and then give the outside a good shine with your shiny cleaner. A spray of club soda makes stainless steel toasters shine spectacularly.

Kettles can be cleaned on the outside with an all-purpose cleaner or a bit of baking soda on a moistened sponge. The interior can get nasty, scaly buildup that needs to be dealt with, or you'll end up with a chunk of the stuff in your teacup. To remove lime deposits, fill the kettle with equal parts white vinegar and water. Bring to a boil and let stand overnight. Then in the morning it will all come out easily. Rinse a few times with fresh water to remove all traces of buildup and white vinegar.

CABINETS AND DRAWERS: INSIDE AND OUT

First things first, you'll likely need to declutter drawers and cupboards before you can actually clean them. Keeping with our relaxed happy-slob style, we'll take this slowly and surely. Add a single drawer or cupboard to your focus-room cleaning every day for a few weeks and maybe an additional one during your clean-for-all tasks. Aim to tackle three separate drawers or cabinets a week.

If you haven't used a utensil or knickknack in more than two years, it's time to say goodbye. Always remember that there are people who can use those kitchen essentials—please donate these items to friends or to charities who need them. Happy slobs are generous folks, after all.

Dollar stores are excellent sources for small baskets and organizers to get your cupboards and kitchen drawers organized. Once you've decluttered an area in your kitchen, reorganize it so it's neater and likely to stay tidy. Give it a good cleaning with a sponge and some all-purpose cleaner and then store things back inside nice and neatly.

To clean cupboards inside and out, use one of our lovely all-purpose sprays and a sponge or cloth. Next time you open a drawer or cabinet you'll be shocked by how clean it is in there! Your family may think they're in the wrong home.

Remember a few keys when reorganizing those nicely decluttered cupboards and cabinets.

- To keep them decluttered, get into the habit of putting away items as soon as you're done with them. It sounds too simple to work, but it will reap great results if you keep with it. This is a fantastic new habit to introduce your family to as well.
- Logical locations—as in, choose a logical spot for that item in your hands. Dishwasher detergent should be as near to the dishwasher as possible. Spices and baking essentials should likewise be stored in a baking section in your cupboards where everything is easy to locate when you're elbow-deep in cake batter.
- Declutter regularly. Make quick decluttering a regular occurrence during your focus-room cleaning. Storage areas in general get messy fast, and a quick decluttering can do wonders to even the messiest spots.

COUNTERTOPS

Declutter countertops by taking a good, hard look at what you keep on them. Do you really use all those appliances on a regular basis? What other clutter has accumulated on the countertops? Keep only the essentials on the countertops to avoid a cluttered feel. Essentials are items you use at least once a week. Store everything else in cupboards.

Cleaning countertops is a breeze with a few squirts of any of our good all-purpose cleaners and a moist rag or sponge. While you're at it, you can quickly wipe down the appliances that did make the cut and are still sitting out in plain view. I'm a huge fan of club soda in a squirt bottle to make those appliances shine.

THE SINK

Keeping the sink emptier makes your whole kitchen look and feel cleaner. Clean it up nicely by using some baking soda in the sink itself; use a scrubby sponge to scrub off all the grime. Rinse that off and then use a shiny cleaner to add sparkle to the taps and the interior of the sink, too. Lovely! The gunky bits around the edges of the sink are easy to remove if you saturate them with a white vinegar/water cleaning solution and let it sit for a while. Use a toothbrush, skewer or toothpick to get under the edge and remove all the muck.

Depending on the type of sink you have, you'll have to employ slightly different cleaning methods and cleaners. The two most common materials used in sinks are stainless steel or porcelain.

Stainless steel sinks can handle harsher cleaners, including naturally acidic white vinegar. You can scrub a stainless steel sink with some baking soda and use white vinegar spray to shine it up at the end. On the other hand, use just baking soda or soapy water to clean porcelain, which is acid resistant but not acid proof. Simply wipe or scrub your pretty porcelain sink with soapy water, rinse clean, and polish up with a cloth or paper towel.

GARBAGE AND RECYCLING

In our home, my husband is in charge of garbage removal. I have to gently remind him sometimes, but, hey, at least he does it without complaining. If you have family or roomies, this is one chore to assign to them because it doesn't take long and it's not that hard. (Plus then you don't have to deal with the stinky mess. Ha!) Remember, always thank your family for helping out.

Stinky garbage cans can be deodorized with generous sprinkles of baking soda in the bottom—I pour a bit in the bottom every time I remove the garbage bag.

Also clean your garbage can occasionally with a soapy water mixture. You can scrub it out with a long-handled scrub brush. Then dump the water outside, rinse out the can and wipe it clean with paper towels.

Recycling takes some organization—you need separate containers for glass, paper, plastic, etc. Large plastic containers should do the job nicely. Check with your municipality on the recycling programs in your local area and then take advantage of these programs and recycle whenever possible. Keep the sorting containers near the garbage so it's just as easy to recycle as it is to throw something away.

11

Rub-a-Dub-Dub: Clean the Room with the Tub

Here's a strange confession for you: I sometimes actually enjoy cleaning the bathroom. Okay, pick yourself up off the floor, please, and let me explain myself. We have this nifty little shower radio in our bathroom that a dear friend gave us as a gift, and I turn that on and get a-scrubbin'. Maybe it's also because we have only one small bathroom to clean, or maybe it's because I feel like taking bubble baths once the bath is sparkling clean...but whatever the reason, sometimes I don't mind cleaning the bathroom one bit. Whatever your opinion on bathroom cleaning, you'll benefit by learning the happy slob's no-hassle methods of cleaning this room.

CODE-RED CLEANING IN...THE BATHROOM

Emergency cleaning to the rescue! Code-red cleaning always starts with impact areas—those areas people see the most in any room, and therefore those areas that have the greatest impact on the overall look of the room. People notice the mirror (because they can't help but look at their gorgeous reflections), the toilet and the countertop the most in the bathroom. Thank heavens for the shower curtain—tuck it neatly closed and carry on. Quickly wipe down the mirror, taps and sink with shiny cleaner and then wipe the counter. Give the inside of the toilet a quick scrub using a toilet brush and a bit of baking soda, and wipe down the outside quickly with a disinfectant such as the Mighty Tea-Tree Cleaner (see page 43). Light a few scented candles for ambience. In just a few minutes your bathroom will look and feel a thousand times better and be ready for any unexpected guests.

THE ROYAL THRONE: TOILET CLEANING

What a regal name for the most unglamorous seating area in your home! Toilet cleaning is never a barrel of laughs, but it's a lot easier if you do it on a regular basis. Then each cleaning is shorter, simpler and less icky.

Here's how I handle the toilet dilemma: As soon as I go into the bathroom to begin cleaning, I pour into the toilet some baking soda—about ¼ cup or so, but there's no need to measure it precisely—and let it sit while I clean the rest of the room. When everything else is clean, I scrub the inside of the toilet with a brush and give it a flush. (Keep one toilet-cleaning brush in a holder behind every toilet in

Toilet cleaning is never a barrel of laughs, but it's easier if you do it regularly.

> Baby shampoo is a gentle, sweet-smelling and effective cleaner for tubs and sinks.

your home. It's a nasty, germy thing you don't want to tote around in your cleaning kit.) Then spray a disinfectant cleaner on the outside of the toilet, including all sides of the seat and the tank, and wipe down the entire surface. Pay particular attention to disinfecting the toilet handle, where a lot of illness-causing germs collect. You may want to use paper towels or disposable disinfecting wipes on the toilet so you can throw away all those nasty germs.

TUBS, SHOWERS, SINKS AND TILES

My favorite way to clean tiles, tubs and sinks is with a very strange cleaner indeed—baby shampoo. The stuff smells sweet and is easy on your skin as you use it, and it also does a fantastic job of cleaning away gunk. Use a damp sponge or rag and pour a bit of baby shampoo on it. (No need to buy the pricey name brands; the generic baby shampoo works just as well for this. There are also now a variety of environmentally friendly, biodegradable baby shampoos to try.) Give the tiles and tub a good scrub, and it will leave the surfaces sparkling. Inexpensive bottles of shower gel or bubble bath do the same thing.

For gunkier messes on these bathroom surfaces, I love a cleaner called Bar Keepers Friend. Despite what its name might suggest, this is a powerful cleaner for bathroom surfaces and for stainless steel cookware, copper and much more. It's an incredibly fine powder that is also all natural as it is derived from rhubarb powder (which makes it nontoxic and biodegradable). Mix the powder with water to create a paste and then use a cleaning cloth or scrubby sponge, and your scrubbing jobs in the bathroom will become far easier.

Getting Gritty with Gruesome Grout

Grout presents a unique cleaning challenge in that it often gets riddled with mildew. Yick! But instead of buying all sorts of expensive cleaners, I have a couple options for you that are happy-slob-worthy. Douse a cotton ball with some hydrogen peroxide and rub it over the mildewy spots. Allow it to sit on the mildewy spots for a few minutes; then use an old toothbrush or small scrub brush to scrub it clean. (You can also invest in an inexpensive grout-cleaning tool, available for a few bucks at most large home stores.) For a little added

An "Airy" Way to Conquer Mildew

Mildew and mold are common problems in the bathroom because the bathroom is a warm, damp environment, which mildew and mold just love. Once you've cleaned away mold or mildew, keep it away longer by airing out the bathroom. If you have an exhaust fan in the bathroom, run it while you are in the bath or shower. Leave the fan running until the humidity leaves the room. Leave the bathroom door open when the room's not in use. Why? Mildew and mold need moisture to thrive. Increasing the air flow will reduce the humidity in the room and help reduce the problem naturally.

cleaning energy on those grout lines, sprinkle some baking soda on the scrub brush before you use it on the peroxide-treated mildew.

THE HAPPY SLOB'S "NEVER CLEAN THE SHOWER AGAIN" PLAN

I can just imagine your repulsed faces and your complaints, "Hey, I may be a happy slob, but I'm not filthy and disgusting!" Wait, wait, and please don't throw away this book—there is a method to my madness. This is how I took the disgusting job of cleaning the shower and made it simply go away in two minutes a day.

When I shower, I have about two minutes or so while my conditioner is doing its work. Two minutes of time that can go toward shining up and cleaning the surfaces all around me. About once a week or so, I'll turn on the shower a few minutes before I'm ready to jump in, and I'll spray the shower and tub with the Very Vinegar Cleaner (see page 44). I close the shower curtain and the bathroom door behind me and let the steam and cleaner work for a few minutes before I jump in.

I have my shower as usual.

You have to shower, so why not get rid of a nasty cleaning job while you're at it?

Then, while my conditioner is working, I take a special *cleaning-only* scrubby sponge tucked away in the shower and dab on some bubble bath, body wash or a bit of shampoo. I scrub the upper part of the shower one day and the lower part the next day. The combination of

the white vinegar spray
and the shampoo seems
to work great together!
While I'm rinsing off my
own soap and condition-
er, I splash water around
liberally to help rinse the
vinegar and soap off the
shower and tub, too.

Anytime your drain begins to slow, remove any visible clog from the top of the drain.

That is it! That is the
secret to never spending
time bent over in the shower again, endlessly scrubbing. It's as much
fun as cleaning gets, and you're in the nude while you do it—very
freeing indeed! You have to shower anyway, so why not get rid of a
nasty cleaning job while you're at it?

NO MORE "DRAINY" DAYS: DRAINS AND CLOGS 101

Smooth-running pipes sounds like a catchphrase from a cheesy
commercial for all-natural fiber laxatives...but, no, we're talking lit
eral pipes here. If you have a nasty clog, no worries! And, if you want
to prevent those clogged pipes in the first place, you've got it!

If the situation is dire, you can go out and buy a heavy-duty
drain declogger at the hardware store. The problem is that these
products can be incredibly toxic—hard on the health of you, your
family and the earth. So white vinegar and baking soda come to the
rescue again! A foamy mix of the two will either unclog backed-up
drains or, with regular use, help prevent those nasty and annoying
clogs from forming in the first place.

Pour ½ cup baking soda down the drain and then follow with

the same amount of white vinegar. Plug the drain immediately! (This will ensure that the foam goes down and works on the problem, not upward and defeating the purpose.) It will foam and cause quite a commotion, so leave it alone for about fifteen minutes or even longer if the clog is a nasty one. In the meantime, fill your teakettle with water and set it to boil. When the fifteen minutes is up, carefully pour the entire kettleful of water down the drain to get it moving safely again. There you go—clear-running drains! And if by chance your drains aren't running as smoothly as you'd like after one application, use the same technique again, letting the white vinegar and baking soda sit and work even longer. (Please note: *Do not* use this method if you've recently used a commercial drain-cleaning product. Harmful vapors may form when the white vinegar and chemicals combine.)

Use this method periodically—before the drain gets clogged—to prevent clogs from happening in the first place. Anytime you notice even a slight slowing of water running down the drain, remove any visible clog from the top of the drain (kitchen skewers work well for this), grab your trusty box of baking soda and your bottle of white vinegar, and get to work!

MIRROR, MIRROR ON THE WALL...

Mirrors are easy to clean with a bunch of old newspapers and a shiny cleaner of your choice—either store-bought or homemade. The Very Vinegar Cleaner (see page 44) or club soda are my favorites. They both work well, and both options are also easy on the wallet. Just spray some on, and use the crumpled papers to wipe it off without a streak or smear in sight. And remember that stale club soda will work just as well as the fresh, bubbly stuff, so it's a great way to use up that long-forgotten bottle tucked away in the back of the fridge.

Floors in bathrooms are often linoleum or tile and just require our good old white-vinegar-and-water solution—Very Vinegar Cleaner—to clean. For more in-depth tips on cleaning these and all other floors, check Chapter 7.

There, now, didn't I tell you cleaning the bathroom isn't as intimidating as you might have thought? With a few tricks and techniques in your cleaning arsenal, you'll be set to clean this room and turn it into your own personal sanctuary. Ahhh…the sheer bliss of it all!

12

"I Prefer to Call it a Lived-in Look": Cleaning Living Areas

One of my favorite new terms over the past decade or so is *shabby chic*. For a long time I used that as a convenient and trendy way to explain the grubbiness of my living room. It's where my husband and I and our two cats spend most of our time. Whether we are lounging around on the floor with newspapers to read (endless fun for our cats, who chew on the edges and attack the papers with glee) or sitting on the sofa curled up with bowls of buttery popcorn watching TV, the living room is…where we live! So it's never going to be a palace of perfection or a habitat of utter serenity. The living areas in our homes are where we all spend most of our time with those we love, and where we laugh and learn and play. So first things first—don't expect perfection!

CODE-RED CLEANING IN...LIVING AREAS

Living areas are, well, lived in! That means they get messy faster and thus are more of a challenge to keep tidy. Again, the way to tackle this chore is to spend any time you can on a quick cleaning of the most noticeable surfaces and a mini decluttering session. Get your family members or roommates involved and make each person responsible for removing his or her items from the room (this could be shoes, clothing, books, toys or craft projects). A large garbage bag will store the junk you don't have time to organize. Throw that garbage bag into any closet far away from peering eyes. (Just remember to note in your cleaning notebook where you put that clutter bag and when you put it there. That way you won't forget about it entirely.) Throw open the window to get some fresh air and vacuum quickly if you have time. A spritz of natural air freshener will provide the finishing touch, if you so choose. Again, our trick of lowering the lights and lighting a few candles adds not only ambience but also helps to hide the mess!

So how can we possibly keep these areas tidy? If they're supposed to look lived in, is it really a problem if they contain all the toys the kids have ever collected? (Yes, and those same kids are off at college now, but what's your point?)

The living areas in our homes are where we spend most of our time.

For help with living areas we need *storage*. Take note of your living areas and the storage you have available to you. Likely the reason those rooms are so cluttered is you have too much stuff and not enough storage to contain it all.

To reduce living-area clutter, you'll need to do the following.

1. *Increase storage:* Provide yourself with plenty of storage—such as shelving units, boxes, baskets, storage containers, etc. For an economic way to add extra storage, purchase a tall, inexpensive bookshelf. Attach a curtain rod at the top of the unit and hang a funky curtain from the rod. You can keep your stuff in there nicely concealed without spending a mint on a new armoire.

2. *Remember to P.A.Y.: Pick up after yourself!* Sorry to get a bit loud there, but it's an obvious rule that we happy slobs have a real problem with. When you're done with that newspaper, put it in the newspaper bin. When you've finished creating some crafty masterpiece, put the craft supplies away in a storage container. When you finish a cup of tea or a bowl of popcorn, take it to the kitchen. This will reduce your cleaning time drastically because most of your stuff will already be where it should be. You'll spend less time picking things up and more time doing meaningful cleaning. And then the next time you're looking for your stuff, it'll be easy to find—saving you an incredible amount of time. (See page 22 for more information on P.A.Y.ing around the house.)

> *Picking up after yourself will reduce your cleaning time drastically.*

3. **Declutter:** If you have way too much stuff, there's no way you can contain it in any organized way. Mark four boxes or bags with KEEP, GIVE AWAY, THROW AWAY and RECYCLE. Get a friend to go through the stuff with you—someone you know will be a bit ruthless and will actually urge you to get rid of junk.

CLEANING UPHOLSTERY AND FURNITURE

The soft furniture in your living area creates a cozy haven for your entire family. Think soft, cushy couches you can fall into with a book...or a comfy chair that almost seems molded to your body contours. They're wonderful! These vital pieces of comfort need occasional cleaning and a little extra attention if there are stains or spots to contend with.

When you vacuum the living areas, occasionally take time to run the upholstery attachment of your trusty vacuum cleaner along the furniture to remove dirt and accumulated dust. Remember to lift up cushions and get at the dust bunnies and stray pieces of popcorn and chips gathering and reproducing under there. Doing this task once in a while (about every month or two) will help with the deeper cleaning of these pieces of furniture later on.

Get a friend to help you go through your stuff and urge you to get rid of junk.

Why Steam it Clean?

What's the big deal about steam cleaning? Whether you're steam cleaning your carpet or your favorite chair, steam cleaning works to deep clean surfaces that otherwise wouldn't get touched. Steam cleaning also helps combat common household allergens like dust mites—the heat of the steam actually kills these nasty little allergens. So if there's a family member with asthma or allergies, steam cleaning should help keep them breathing easier.

If you're the sort who gets a professional to come in to do the carpet cleaning, ask about their upholstery-cleaning services. For an additional fee, these pros can quickly and efficiently clean your upholstered surfaces along with the carpet in your home. On the other hand, if you've gone ahead and purchased a carpet steam cleaner (or plan on renting one occasionally), you can use this to clean upholstered furniture like sofas, cushy chairs and ottomans. If you have any doubt about the durability of the fabric on your upholstered furniture, test an inconspicuous spot first to make sure it can handle the steam cleaning. Steam cleaning will spruce up the overall look of your furniture, but if there are stains, you'll need to pretreat these with furniture stain or spot remover (available in the same spot the steam-cleaning fluid is).

On most new pieces of furniture you have an option to get a protective stain-repellent treatment applied to the fabric. Overall, I think this is money very well spent! For our new sofa and chair I had this stain treatment applied, and now stains are as easy to clean as a dab-dab-dab with a dampened sponge or cloth. It really has made an incredible difference.

Now you're ready to tidy up the most loved and lived-in areas in your home. For even more helpful tips on cleaning living rooms and living areas, check out Chapter 7 on floor cleaning, Chapter 8 on cleaning walls and windows and Chapter 9 on dusting. You're all set, you cleaning machine, you!

13
Snuggles and Snoozes: Cleaning Bedrooms and Closets

Oh, sweet bedroom! How we love thee! You are our romantic, beckoning hideaway where we can truly relax and are comforted and consoled into long, luxurious sleeps all nestled in our pristine, fluffy white beds. Ahhh, sweet serenity...

Reality check! Is your bedroom more of a horror movie than a hideaway? Is it more cringe-inducing than snooze-inducing? Okay, well, you've found the right chapter to conquer the clutter and over-all disarray of your bedroom. By the time you're finished with this chapter, you'll be well on your way to a happier, cozier little retreat you can truly call your own. And, yes, that includes tackling terrifying closets while we're at it. They're not so big or bad when you're ready for them.

CODE-RED CLEANING IN...THE BEDROOM

Your closets are a *great* place to toss junk if unexpected guests arrive. Spend your time making the bed. (This is where the suggestions found later in the chapter on keeping bed linens to a minimum *really* help.) Do a quick vacuum if you have time and dust really quickly. Junk and clutter can be tossed into a large garbage bag and stored in the closet. Close those closet doors tightly—we don't want any snoops taking a peek now, do we?

To ensure those clutter bags aren't lost forever in the continuum of clutter, take a brief moment to jot down the date and location you put them in. (This is where your cleaning notebook comes in handy, yet again.) Just a quick note will allow you to work on this area later during one of your weekly clean-for-alls.

For a nice extra touch, spray some scented room spray in a soothing scent like lavender or citrus to finish off the room or just throw open a window and air it out. Plump up some throw cushions on top of the freshly made bed, and that's it, you've done it! No guest can intimidate you, you great cleaning fiend.

DO YOU MAKE THE BED EVERY DAY?

Raise your hand if you make your bed every day. That's what I thought, not many of us happy slobs are the best or most consistent bed makers. To be frank, I'd be a bit disappointed and shocked if you were! Sometimes it just doesn't make sense to make the bed: If you're lounging around on a Sunday morning with bagels and coffee and newspapers to peruse, or travel

Most days it makes sense to make the bed. It looks tidy, and it helps us relax.

brochures to flip through and drool over, making the bed wrecks the sweet, laid-back mood. Or if you aren't feeling well or you need to crawl into bed for a sustaining afternoon nap, why make the bed? It's a waste of time and energy.

But most days it makes sense to make the bed. It looks tidy, but even more importantly, it helps us relax. Think I'm crazy? Think again. You are reading this book to learn how to clean and contain clutter. And I'm guessing part of the reason you want to clean is the mess likely makes you feel stressed. Those ever-growing piles of junk and clutter can stifle anyone's enthusiasm and, worse, can be an exercise in anxiety. So little changes—like getting into the habit of making your bed most days—can gradually chip away at those worrisome thoughts.

There is nothing nicer at the end of a hectic day than coming home to a neatly made bed with mounds of fluffy cushions—it

Five or Under

Take out your trusty timer again because you're about to prove another cleaning point to yourself. No more whining and complaining about how long it takes to make the bed! If you keep the bedding simple, making your bed should seriously not take any longer than five minutes—three minutes tops when you get used to making the bed every day. Okay, go ahead! Time yourself. Three to five minutes each morning is not a big sacrifice for decreasing stress overall. And the next time you catch yourself whining about making the bed, remind yourself that anyone can endure three to five minutes. And that includes you and me, my fellow happy slob.

seems to invite you to crawl in to relax. A bed piled with books, bills and a cluster of tangled linens isn't nearly as welcoming. It just adds to the stress of an already long and tiring day. Your bedroom and your bed in particular should be a sanctuary at the end

> *Your bedroom should be a sanctuary at the end of the day.*

of the day. I know that sounds cheesy, but give it a try and see for yourself if it doesn't actually make you feel more relaxed.

To make the bed, simply remove everything but the fitted sheet. Tidy that up by smoothing it out. Add the flat sheet on top, tucking it under, and then add the fluffy duvet on top of that. The final touches are to add the pillows and cushions—as many as you like! But don't go too pillow crazy, or it just wastes time to sort them every morning. Don't worry about crisp hospital corners. As long as your bed is neatly made, that's good enough. You don't live in an institution so you don't need perfect bed making skills. It's the cozy little haven you sleep in, not an area that undergoes daily inspection, after all.

K.L.S.S.: Keep Linens Simple, Slob!

If you hate bed making but are determined to give it a try, keep this in mind: Keep the linens simple! Simple equals streamlined. A bed with a couple sheets (one flat, one fitted) and a duvet on top is as simple as it gets. Add a couple pillows with fun pillowcases, and

✱ Air it Out

Take a few minutes in the morning to give your bed time to take a deep breath, as it were, by airing your bedding out. If it isn't freezing outside, open a window wide and pull back the blankets and sheets, and if you're so inclined you can even spray a bit of natural linen spray on the sheets. While you're showering or eating breakfast, let the bed air out a bit...and then take all of three minutes or so to quickly make the bed. You'll be glad later on that you did!

you're set! Layers and layers of linens might feel ultraluxurious when you crawl into bed at night, but they sure do create a hassle every morning when it's time to make the bed again. You'll be relieved then that you kept things simple.

Duvets are not only great big fluffy clouds of comfort, they're also great at hiding rumpled or wrinkled sheets beneath. So even if you had only a minute to whip together the bed this morning, that handy duvet will hide the incriminating evidence perfectly.

If, like me, you live in a cold climate, you'll need to add an extra blanket or two in the fall and winter for pure warmth. Otherwise, stick with the simple sheets-and-duvet method. It looks good, it's fluffy and cozy, and it's ridiculously easy to maintain. And that is a concept we happy slobs embrace wholeheartedly.

CLEAN IT RIGHT: BEDROOMS

Of course, there is more involved in cleaning your bedroom than just making the bed. Look all around and then up and down, and you'll clearly see the other areas that also need a bit of attention.

We're talking about floors, windows, walls and other surfaces like your furniture. For down-and-dirty information on these vital areas in your bedrooms, check

- Chapter 7 on cleaning floors.
- Chapter 8 on walls and windows.
- Chapter 9 on dusting.
- Chapter 15 on tips laundry.

And don't forget, one of the easiest ways to keep your bedroom clean is to remember to P.A.Y., as in pick up after yourself (see page 22 for more on this idea).

Organizing Tools for Bedrooms

You won't necessarily need all these organizers, but having at least a few on hand will greatly increase the organization in your bedroom. By having homes for your stuff—shelves for books, boxes for jewelry, etc.—you'll have more success keeping your bedroom tidy and cozy.

- **Boxes with lids and labels:** Useful in a thousand and one ways. Great for storing clothes, photo albums, keepsakes, etc. Labeling the boxes makes it easy to find your stuff later on.
- **Closet organizers:** Adjustable rods, racks, drawers and bins have made the modern closet one of überorganization! No need to go crazy with this, but a few well-thought-out additions to your closet can greatly increase the usable space within (and therefore keeping it tidier) and give you more space for new clothes, which is never a bad thing.
- **Dresser inserts:** These clever little inventions can help fully utilize your dresser space. Great for organizing small items like undies or socks.

Linens Lost and Found

After washing sheets and pillowcases, tuck the matching clean sheets into the pillowcases immediately. Then the next time you change the sheets, everything you need is together in one convenient bundle— easy to get the job done. And no more time wasted searching for this pillowcase and that sheet. Those few extra minutes saved can be used to get the chore of making the bed over and done with.

- *Jewelry boxes:* Ooh, look at your glam style! Keep all your jewelry in one easy-to-access spot with a jewelry box.
- *Laundry bags or baskets:* This is a must-have! Instead of letting the laundry mosey all over your bedroom and create chaos, keep it all in one spot—a laundry bag or basket. Some laundry baskets have divided sections so you can sort clothes as you go—colorful clothing in one section and whites in another.
- *Makeup organizer:* All your beautifying solutions in one spot. It makes getting ready a lot simpler and faster. For guys, a toiletry bag or organizer will do the same thing.
- *Shelves:* For more than just books! Adding shelves in the bedroom instantly adds storage space. Boxes or baskets on shelves is a great pairing—an easy way to store your stuff but still conceal it all the while.
- *Shoe racks:* Vital for any shoe lover. There is a wide variety available, from behind-the-door hanging types to great big closet inserts that hold dozens of pairs.

- **Tie racks:** Useful for more than just ties. Great for scarves and belts, too. Some women swear by them for organizing necklaces and other jewelry as well.

BE BRAVE, NOW...CLOSETS AND OTHER STORAGE AREAS

The closet may be the messiest part of your bedroom, but don't worry, we'll tame that cleaning beast the no-hassle way.

Why we love them: We love closets because they are the best hiding places for clutter and mess.

And, of course, these areas are where we keep all our favorite things, so closets are actually a happy slob's greatest pals, after our cleaning kits.

Why we hate them: They're where we love to hide our clutter and mess—and so they can become overwhelmingly disastrous!

Bit-by-Bit Closet Cleaning

Most of us happy slobs have neither the time nor the inclination to sit down on a Saturday afternoon to clean out an entire horrible closet. But add a simple goal every day to your cleaning bursts—say that you'll remove or organize five items every day from one closet—and you'll be surprised how quickly and easily you'll accomplish your goals. Once that first closet is tidier, move on to another one.

Your closet may be messy but don't worry, we'll tame it the no-hassle way!

Or, if you're feeling more motivated, break the closet cleaning into sections. For instance, clean the *top* of the closet one time, and then the next time you can clean the *middle* and then finally the *bottom*. This way you won't feel so overwhelmed and frustrated when you're in the middle of cleaning the entire thing and it feels like it will take years to get the job done.

The most important thing is to avoid organizing burnout. When we get the organizing bug, we tend to go overboard and burn ourselves out completely. And then we decide never to organize anything ever again! (Don't you love how balanced we happy slobs are? Oh, dear.) Instead, chop up large organizing tasks into smaller, easy-to-manage bits.

> *When we get the organizing bug, we tend to go overboard and burn out.*

Help for Your Bedroom Closet

- **Don't overstuff your closets.** Get rid of old clothes you haven't worn in years; charities or friends will be glad for your contributions. (I love when friends go on organizing binges. I get a whole new assortment of clothes for free—how much better could that be?)
- **Organize your closets in a logical way.** If you wear that black jacket only a couple times a year, put it near the back or the top of your closet. Your everyday wear—the essential clothes

you wear over and over—should be easily accessible and within reach.

- **Shoe racks** on the closet floor will help keep your shoes from becoming a jumbled pile. No more searching for your favorite pair. (If you run out of room in the closet, check out under-the-bed shoe storage units. They're a fantastic use of under-utilized space. Or you can find shoe organizers that hang from the closet rod.)
- **Sort clothing according to season.** Pack away similar types of clothing in bags and boxes. For example, all the summer shirts go together, as do the heavy sweaters, etc. Pull these out only when you need them for that season.
- **Sort your clothing in specific outfits** to make getting dressed every morning fast and easy.
- **Use stackable, clear plastic storage containers** on your top shelves so you can easily see what's inside. You can also add a label on each to make it even easier to find what you're looking for: one box for sweatshirts, one for tees, one for jeans, etc.
- **Store empty hangers in a clear plastic bin.** It'll be easy to find one when you need it (such as when you're ironing), and it'll clear up a lot of much-needed space in your closet.

INCREASE YOUR STORAGE SPACE

It's a sad reality that many of our homes aren't fitted with enough storage, so it's a challenge to keep things organized. Here are some tips to help.

1. Have you worn that in two years? Clear out those old items! You'll be shocked by how much space you gain. And, no, those seventies bellbottoms likely won't come back in style.

2. Every bit of space counts, which means organizing the top, middle and bottom of every closet. Storage boxes or stacking wire organizers on the top means you can store sweaters and T-shirts up there easily. Hooks on the walls of closets allow you to neatly organize accessories such as handbags and scarves or ties. Use shoe racks on the floor to optimize shoe storage.

3. Create simple additional storage space by using a tall, inexpensive bookcase, and cover the front with a funky curtain to match the colors in your bedroom. Voilà, extra storage, neatly concealed!

4. Hidden potential: under-the-bed storage. Often forgotten, this is underutilized storage space. You can get specially designed under-bed boxes that are flat and long and are great for clothing you don't wear on a regular basis or for extra linens that don't fit in the linen closet.

5. If you add, also subtract. Organizing experts keep telling us happy slobs we need to remove old items from our closets whenever we add new ones. If you buy two new pieces of clothing, remove two old pieces from your closet before adding the new items. It'll keep your closet from becoming a disaster zone!

6. Get inspired. For organizing inspiration, visit a storage solutions store. Whenever I walk into an organizing shop, I feel the urge to go home and organize all my cluttered areas. (That feeling, sadly, is usually far less intense by the time I reach home again.) You'll find incredible solutions for storage and organizing issues in any area of your home.

Remember our goal at the outset of this chapter? To turn our unappealing bedrooms into havens of rest and tranquillity? It really isn't an impossible task, and now you'll be developing great new habits quickly and easily. Lots of little efforts equal huge successes! In no time your bedroom will be your favorite room, not just a pit you walk into only in the dark of night to flop into bed. You should be set to make the bed (almost) every day, handle emergency cleaning situations and even confront the closets. I am so proud of you, I could burst. But instead I'll just eat a chunk of chocolate to celebrate your progress. It's less painful altogether.

14

Hope for the Home Office

Hurray for the home office! It's where all sorts of important work gets carried out—from handling family finances to developing new business ideas to…ahem…carrying out important spy missions via your favorite computer game. Whatever your family uses the home office for, one glance around the piles of files and seemingly never-ending papers and books will convince even the most laid back of happy slobs that it's time to take a little action. And so we shall!

CODE-RED CLEANING IN…THE OFFICE

A visitor is on the way—maybe even a (gasp!) client—and you need to clean up the clutter in your office fast! Get out your cleaning kit quickly. Do a speedy dusting and put piles of unnecessary clutter into a large garbage bag; stow in a closet to deal with later. (As always, be sure to take note in your cleaning notebook of when and where you put these clutter bags. Otherwise they'll be easy to forget about forever. Conquer the clutter bags the next time you're in that particular room for a focus-room cleaning.) A quick cleaning with an all-purpose cleaner and a rag will do wonders to dust and spruce up the place. If you have time, run the vacuum quickly and empty out the garbage. Open a window, if the weather is nice, to air the place out. Have coffee and goodies ready for visitors when they arrive, and they won't notice anything else.

As a somewhat-functioning freelance writer, I'm fortunate enough to work from home. In fact, my "home office" is about two steps away from my bed (great for middle-of-assignment naps when I can't bear to look at that horrible, blinking cursor for one more second). There are definite benefits to working at home, but there are some serious downfalls, too. The number-one culprit in our home offices is clutter!

The number one culprit in our home offices is clutter!

Like we already talked about in our living areas, we need adequate *storage* to contain our stuff. Without anywhere to put things, we'll be running on an endless clutter wheel with no way to disembark.

TEN TIPS TO ORGANIZED HOME OFFICES

Yes, I used that nasty word *organized* again. But even we happy slobs can learn to be more organized in a fairly painless way. And minus the hassle!

1. *Declutter every week.* Pick one day every week to spend at least ten minutes organizing and decluttering your desk. (I like Fridays because the weekend is nearly here, and I'm feeling pretty darn positive!) Throw out the garbage, take out the recyclables, deal with files, etc.

2. *Set up a paperwork solution.* Again, if you have nowhere to put your bills, receipts and other important papers, you can't possibly get organized. Set up a filing system that works for you. If you're really lost, enlist the help of a more organized friend to help you get set up. Create a "to-file" box to contain your paperwork during the week; then at the end of the week sort all the papers in a frenzy of filing. You'll still get all the essential filing work completed, but it'll take less time overall. (Do your weekly filing during your weekly decluttering session.)

3. *It's done!* At the conclusion of each project, immediately put appropriate papers into your "to-file" box to file at the end of the week. This will prevent piles of paper from accumulating on your desk.

4. *Cute containers and organizers.* Visit an office supply store to get new organizers, mail trays and desk drawer dividers to help keep everything in its place so it's easy to find what you need right when you need it—whatever "it" happens to be!

5. *Masses of mail.* Place a garbage can and recycling bin near where you open your daily mail. This makes it easier to deal with papers right away—instead of letting them grow into scary reproducing piles all over your office.

6. *Efficient computer files.* Nowadays many of our files are electronic ones. If you waste valuable time searching for these,

start working a few minutes every day on transferring files into new electronic file folders that are more user-friendly.

7. *Utilize wall space.* None of us has as much space as we'd like, so utilize that valuable wall space! Shelves, hooks or organizers can all be adhered to the wall. Again, a visit to an office supply store will provide you with plenty of selection. (Remember to take lots of measurements of the space you're gearing out with new shelves and organizing containers. Jot it all down in a notebook so you don't buy shelves that won't fit your space. And take a measuring tape with you to the store to make further measurements.)

8. *Create business hours.* Let the whole family know when your business hours are, even though you're working from home. This helps you organize your time more efficiently—it's a lot easier to do when the kids aren't popping in every five minutes to ask you questions. Now, if only cats would respect such rules!

Vacuuming No-No

Although grabbing your trusty vacuum to clean out the inner workings of your computer might seem like the most logical thing in the world, don't do it! The static discharge can harm your computer's tube and eventually cause the computer to fail altogether. If you feel confident about cleaning inside your computer, opt for small cans of compressed air available in any computer store—or even a turkey baster (minus the rich gravy) can gently blow air onto delicate parts to remove built-up dust.

9. **Schedule your time.** It's obvious, but do you use a daily journal to budget your time? Don't make it too strict, as life has this funny way of messing up the best-laid plans—but do list at least a couple different projects you want to focus on each day.

10. **Office cleaning kit.** Just a small cleaning kit with essentials like cleaning cloths, all-purpose cleaning spray and a duster will do the trick. It's great for quick cleanups or when a client is coming over at the last minute. And keep a window open in the office whenever possible. Natural birdsong and the cool breezes flowing through the window will help you relax and be more productive.

CLEANING THE COMPUTER SAFELY

Here is one cleaning task that not just anyone can perform. You can clean your keyboard and monitor yourself (no chemicals, please—just a lint-free cloth for the monitor and a can of compressed air to force out dust from between keyboard keys), but you'll need a pro to clean inside your computer. Ask a technically knowledgeable friend about opening up the computer to clean in there once in a while because you'd be shocked by how many dust bunnies collect inside for family reunions. I was grossed out when I saw inside my computer for the first time. And here I'd thought under the bed was bad!

Have the inside of your computer cleaned once or twice a year. Too much dust accumulating on the components inside the computer can cause damage. *But* remember that dusting inside your computer in an incorrect way can cause far *more* damage. That's why I highly recommend getting a pro to do the job if you doubt in any way that you can do it yourself. Help prevent some of the dust in the

That Keyboard is a Colony

On a diet? Well, this information will definitely put you off food for a while! (You can thank me later.) That keyboard of yours is teeming with germs. In fact, lab tests have proven that your keyboard can contain five times more germs than a typical toilet seat. So this is one instance when I think natural disinfecting wipes come in very handy. Keep a packet in a desk drawer and wipe down the keyboard and mouse when you do your weekly desk decluttering.

first place by purchasing computer air filters at computer specialty stores. (Some online computer pros even suggest squares of clean panty hose! It's a cheap solution, and you can simply replace them every month or so.) You can hire a computer-cleaning specialist by checking a phone book. Or simply call a computer store and ask whom they'd recommend. Having computer-geek pals really comes in handy when you want to clean out your computer—just bribe them with a new video game, and they'll be putty in your hands.

See, even if you work from home, you can keep your office looking spiffy and professional. It'll not only impress potential clients, it'll inspire you to greater feats of creativity and productivity. Use these cleaning and organizing tips—especially the weekly ten-minute declutter—to keep piles of files from taking over. Take back your workspace with these handy hints and good habits!

15

Lovin' Laundry— You (Almost) Will

Remember that cozy feeling when Mom would do a fresh load of laundry? You'd grab your favorite comfy pajamas while they were still warm and smelled like springtime breezes. (Okay, at least in my memory they did. Stop that scoffing! In your memory of childhood they can smell like whatever you want them to.) Such memories of warm, comfortingly clean clothes make even the most laid-back happy slobs eager to learn at least the basics of effectively washing laundry. And so you shall! Getting your clothes clean isn't nearly as complicated as you might think, and I've got loads (pun intended, thank you) of ideas to make it easier than ever. Consider this chapter your guide to laundry, dehassled!

CHOOSING A LAUNDRY DAY

Before we get into the nitty-gritty of laundry, it's important to choose a day when you can focus on doing this thrilling household task. If, like me, you don't have a washer and drier of your very own, you should learn when the local Laundromat or your apartment's laundry rooms are the least busy so you can get the most accomplished in the shortest amount of time. Because I work from home, I can do my laundry on Tuesday or Wednesday mornings and afternoons, which is the quietest time around these here parts.

If, on the other hand, you have your own washer and drier, you can choose whichever days work best for you and your family. Many love Sundays—just before the dawn of the new week, thus preparing you for the week ahead. Choose a laundry day that works for you and try your best to stick to it. Otherwise, if your family goes through a lot of laundry, you'll want to just pop in a load whenever the laundry basket is full.

SORTING

Sorting is a vital step when doing laundry unless you really want all of your stylish, sparkling white T-shirts to come out a pretty pastel shade of pink, which is what happens when you mistakenly toss a red shirt in with the whites. We've all done this, but it's an easy mistake to prevent.

*Don't Overload It

Don't overload the washing machine! We're all tempted to do this so we can get all our dirty laundry washed quickly, but it won't clean your clothes as well as if you didn't overload. Plus, it may cause the washer to overflow, just making more mess to clean. And that would defeat the purpose altogether, now, wouldn't it?

Which Cycle to Choose?

- **Whites:** Regular wash cycle, hot water temperature, normal drier setting

- **Colors:** Regular wash cycle, warm/cold water temperature, normal drier setting

- **Permanent press:** Permanent-press wash cycle, cold water temperature, permanent-press drier setting

- **Delicates:** Delicates wash cycle, cold water temperature, delicate drier setting or line dry

- **Wool:** Delicates wash cycle, cold water temperature, tumble dry/no-heat drier setting

You'll need to sort your clothes into three different groups: whites, colors and delicates. You can purchase groovy laundry organizers with built-in dividers or just use three laundry bags or baskets.

I know you might not see the point of sorting laundry, but your whites will look a hundred times nicer if you clean them separately in hot water with either bleach or a bleach alternative. Your colors will retain their crisp hues when washed on their own, and your delicates will stay in one piece.

DETERGENTS, BLEACH AND MORE

I'm a huge fan of liquid laundry detergent for two major reason—it doesn't leave those awful, clumpy bits of powder all over your clothes, nor does it leave any shadowy residue. Liquid detergent tends to be a bit more expensive, so if you must, you can still use powder. But I highly recommend buying the liquid detergent when it's on sale. It works as a pretreatment, too, thus sparing you the cost of buying separate stain removers.

When You Run out of Detergent...

Guess what else you can use to clean your clothes? Inexpensive shampoo! This works surprisingly well. Just use a few capfuls for the wash and then plain white vinegar as a fabric softener. Baby shampoo is especially mild. This makes a great replacement when you don't have any detergent left and you really need to do a load of laundry.

Bleach and Bleach Alternatives

There's a great ongoing debate about using bleach. Chlorine bleach is irritating to the lungs and eyes and contains some toxic chemicals. Ammonia is also a strong eye and lung irritant, so I like to stay away from these as much as possible. If you or anyone in your family has asthma or other breathing problems, you should not clean with bleach or ammonia.

Earth-Friendly Laundry

Many of us are very concerned about the effect phosphates and other ingredients in common laundry detergents have on the environment. But there's good news! At your local supermarket you can easily find newer-generation detergents that contain natural ingredients and are phosphate free, so you get cleaner clothes with a lighter conscience.

Try one of these bleach alternatives added to the wash instead (but don't mix them together):

- ½ to 1 cup of borax
- 1 cup of white vinegar
- ½ to 1 cup baking soda

Fabric Softener

Adding white vinegar helps soften clothes in place of fabric softeners. Add about a cup of white vinegar to your load during the rinse cycle. Or pour about a tablespoon or so of liquid fabric softener on a clean face cloth and toss it in the drier like you would any fabric-softener sheet. It makes a bottle last just about forever!

STAIN REMOVAL

For everyday stains, use baby shampoo and a soft, clean toothbrush to pretreat stains and then launder as usual. A 50/50 white vinegar to water solution also works great on stains—just spray on, scrub gently with a soft toothbrush and let sit before washing. Other tough stains, such as spaghetti sauce, come out well if you use a paste made from a bit of dishwashing detergent or baking soda and a little water. Rub with a toothbrush and then pop in the wash cycle.

Note: Be sure to check the garment's label before going

Shampoo makes a handy detergent substitute if you happen to run out.

ahead with any type of stain removal. Certain fabrics are strictly dry-clean only, and you can damage the clothing irreparably if you go ahead and try to take the stain out yourself. Tell the dry cleaner about what type of stain it is and how long it's been there—all the details will help them battle the stain more effectively.

Stain Removal Must-Haves

- **Cold water:** Never use hot water to get out stains, as the heat will actually help set the stain—not what you had in mind. Instead use cold tap water to help take out that nasty stain.
- **Hydrogen peroxide:** Fantastic at removing stains, but remember: Hydrogen peroxide basically acts as bleach. So on white garments you should be safe, but on colorful fabrics, be very careful and test the fabric first in an inconspicuous spot.
- **Hairspray:** Well known as a great ink-stain remover.
- **Liquid laundry detergent:** As mentioned earlier, buying liquid laundry detergent is in effect buying two products in one. A little of this stuff on stains or ring-around-the-collar works better than many commercial stain lifters. Just gently scrub it in, using a soft toothbrush or other type of cleaning brush, and let it sit and work for about ten minutes before putting it in the washing machine.
- **Shampoo:** Like liquid laundry detergent, this is a fabulous all-purpose stain lifter on many organic stains. And it's mild—so give it a try! (It's also a handy detergent substitute if you've happened to run out.)
- **Toothbrush or other small scrubber:** To gently scrub out that stain! Make sure the brush is soft; if the bristles are too hard, they could damage the fabric.

Try and Try Again

Many stains will take a few applications before they are fully removed, so don't be frustrated if that stain hasn't totally disappeared the first time around. Just try again—or possibly three times—and you should be able to remove many stains. Despite your best efforts, however, some stains may be stuck for life.

- **Washing machine:** That's right, this is one of your best tools in getting out stains permanently. Once you've pretreated the stain by hand, washing the garment will help to remove that stain for good.

Rinse That Stain Right Out

I can hardly think of any stain that won't benefit from first being rinsed out with cold water. If you do this while the stain is fresh, you'll remove much of the stain before you even have to try these other techniques for removing specific stains.

- **Blood (and other organic stains):** Hydrogen peroxide is a great option here, but only if the fabric is pale or white. Pour it directly onto the stain, let it bubble and then scrub gently. Rinse with cold water and continue the process until all lingering traces are removed. Launder as usual.
- **Coffee or tea:** Try to rinse out as much of the fresh stain as possible with cold water and then dab out the stain with a dry cloth. Pretreat the area with liquid laundry detergent, let sit for about ten minutes to work into the fabric and then launder as usual.

- **Grass:** Ooh, the bane of every mother around the world! Grass stains are especially tricky because they're made up of a complex assortment of proteins. The best bet is to brush off any remaining bits of grass and then pretreat with a liquid or powder laundry detergent, scrubbing it into the stain and allowing it to work a bit before laundering. You'll likely have to repeat this process.

- **Ink:** Ink is likely one of the most difficult stains to remove, but give it a good try. Saturate the stain with regular hairspray (alcohol-based) and use a soft, clean toothbrush to gently rub the stain away. It will likely take a few applications before you see progress; afterward, launder as usual.

- **Wine:** You can purchase red-wine stain removers at many liquor stores or kitchen shops. (I've heard those stain removers are also good for removing blood stains.) One study concluded that hydrogen peroxide mixed with an equal part of Dawn liquid dishwashing detergent was the very best red-wine stain lifter. But remember that hydrogen peroxide works as a bleaching agent, so be careful to test in an inconspicuous spot first, or you might lift away the dye of the garment along with the stain.

Speed Counts

The faster you act to get rid of any stain, the better your chance of getting rid of that stain for good. Keep a few of the common stain-fighting agents on hand so you're stocked and ready to fight stains when and where they happen.

DEALING WITH IT ONCE IT'S DONE

Put the timer on whenever you put clothes in the washer or drier. This enables you to get your clothes out of the drier as soon as the cycle is done—one of the most important ways to avoid ironing. Fold or hang up the items as soon as you can after they're finished drying.

The Colorful-Laundry-Basket System

Each member of your household should be assigned a laundry basket of a different color. Then, when laundry is done, their clothing is piled into their own baskets, and it is their responsibility to put their own laundry away. (Only very young children can't do this.) Always keep these basket colors the same so everyone knows what their laundry basket color is—it will reduce stress on laundry day. And, hey, I know you need less stress in your life.

> *Remove clothes from the drier as soon as the cycle is done to avoid wrinkles.*

AVOID IRONING!

Here's how:

- Choose clothes that wrinkle less (especially when traveling)! Pure cotton clothes tend to wrinkle the most.
- Try a hand-held steamer. Just hang your clothes on hangers and use a steamer to steam out the wrinkles.

- Use the permanent-press cycle in both the washer and drier whenever possible. It prevents wrinkles in your clothing.
- Don't overload the washing machine—too many clothes create pressure and weight and add more wrinkles.
- Remove clothes as soon as they're done tumbling in the drier. Clothes sitting on top of one another create loads of nasty wrinkles.
- An easy way to dewrinkle a garment without pulling out the iron is to lightly mist the clothing with water and then let it sit overnight on a hanger to dry. The wrinkles will naturally release as the garment dries. Your clothing will be ready for you to wear as if the ironing were done for you as you slept. What could be easier!

OR...IF YOU MUST IRON...

If you don't hate ironing as much as I do, you can make your own starch spray for crisper clothes.

Homemade Starch Spray

1 tbsp. cornstarch

1 cup very hot water

Mix together well to allow the cornstarch to completely dissolve. Let cool and then pour into an awaiting spray bottle with a fine-mist setting. Shake mixture well before each and every use. Spray lightly on shirts before ironing for an extra-crisp finish. This recipe works best on white or light fabrics. For darker fabrics, stick with a commercial spray starch, commonly available in the laundry aisle of your favorite supermarket.

Chic Shirts with Less Effort

Can't be bothered with the fuss and muss of properly ironing and starching dress shirts? Take them to the dry cleaner's! The regular price is around two or three bucks a shirt, and on sale it can be half that price. You might consider it money well spent for great-looking shirts without the bother.

Ironing 101

So all happy slobs hate ironing. That is an absolute fact of which we're well aware. But the sad point remains that sometimes you will need to bring out the dreaded appliance and ironing board and iron something. Some people even like ironing—can you imagine it? (Although I must say it would make life a lot easier if I looked forward with great anticipation to ironing a huge mound of laundry!) Anyway, if ironing is a must, here are a few tips to make it an easier and less stressful endeavor overall.

1. ***Better irons = better ironing.*** If you're still using the old behemoth your mother-in-law gave you twenty years ago as a "not-so-subtle" hint, maybe it's time to invest in a new iron. These days, irons are lighter, easier to use, pump out more steam and basically make ironing an easier task altogether. Hurray! Give a new model a try, and you may change your opinion of this dreaded chore.

2. ***Steam it up!*** A lot of steam power will work wonders on many fabrics, helping to release wrinkles. Choose a steam iron with a wide variety of settings to end up with the best results.

3. **Dampen the fabric, not your enthusiasm.** Fabric still slightly wet is far easier to iron to a crisp finish. You can either remove laundry from the drier (or clothesline) while still slightly damp or use a spray bottle to lightly mist the clothing before ironing.

4. **Don't be bored with the board.** If you don't already have one, you'll need to invest in an ironing board. It should be good and sturdy and come complete with a cover, which can be removed and washed once in a while. The ironing board's unique shape makes it easy to iron different types of clothes, whatever crazy angles they might contain.

Fabric still slightly wet will be far easier to iron to a crisp finish.

The wider end is useful for large areas of your clothing such as full skirts or the backs of shirts. The tapered end is for more detailed areas such as collars and cuffs.

5. **Read the labels.** Some garments have very specific guidelines about which setting you should use to iron them. Too hot a setting can scorch a beloved garment, while too low a setting won't get much accomplished at all. Be sure to read the labels.

6. **Presorting prevents problems.** Try saying that ten times in a row! But the fact is that presorting the clothes you need to

How Hot Depends on the Fabric

You don't need to guess which heat setting will work for which type of fabric—your iron will show you the way. There are different settings specifically for a wide range of fabric types. Lowest heat settings are generally for nylon, silk, and acrylic; medium for polyester; higher settings for wool, cotton and linen.

iron will make things much easier as you go along. Presort according to the heat level you'll need to iron them with—lower heat first, such as silks and acrylics, and then edging up to a higher heat for fabrics like linen and wool.

7. **Be cool and then get hot.** It makes sense to start off with the lowest setting of heat you need for more delicate clothing and then gradually increase the heat.

8. **Clean out the iron.** Once in a while, that is. If you notice your iron isn't as steamy and effective as it once was, the iron might need a good clean from the inside out. Fill the iron halfway with white vinegar and then top off with tap water. Turn on the iron and set it to a steam setting. Let it sit and get steamy for about five minutes. Unplug the iron and let cool and then let the iron sit face-side down in some sort of baking dish until all the water/white vinegar mixture has drained out. Fill and refill a few times more with fresh, clean water to flush the whole thing out. Use cotton-tipped swabs to carefully clean the steam vents on the bottom of the iron. (Nothing sharp—you could damage the finish.) Now use your freshly cleaned iron as usual. Double-check with the

manufacturer to make sure you should clean the iron. Some newer models are designed to never be cleaned.

9. **Safety first.** Be extra careful using the iron, especially if you have little children or curious pets around your place. The iron gets incredibly hot and can burn them badly. Keep the iron on only when you're right there to monitor that every-thing—and everyone—is safe. And even if you don't have kids or pets, be careful—an unattended iron could fall over and scorch something.

Are you sure you're a happy slob at all? You're looking very sharp in your crisp-white, freshly pressed shirt! Dressed to impress, I must say. Now could you please come over and iron my laundry for me?

16

Stain Removal 101: Getting out of What You Got Into

Ooh, look at you! All dressed up in your finest for that special night out…when out of the blue drops a mystery stain from the sky to land right on your lapel! Okay, so maybe mystery stains aren't *quite* as mysterious as that, but a stubborn stain makes even the most relaxed of us happy slobs furious.

CARPETS AND UPHOLSTERY

You don't always need the services of a carpet-cleaning company to get out stubborn carpet stains. Sometimes common household products will do the job just as well.

The best way to remove any stain is to fight it when it's fresh. So if a clumsy guest happens to dump a glass of red wine on your creamy ivory carpet, get to work immediately! No more chitchat; it's time for the club soda.

Yet many stains are old, nasty ones that have been around forever and seem as familiar to us as family. Like family, these can be especially tough to budge! Here's a great all-purpose carpet-cleaning solution that uses regular household ingredients: half white vinegar and half water mixed in a spray bottle. Blot up as much of the stain as you can first and then spray with the white vinegar/water mixture. Lay down a few layers of paper towels and a heavy object, such as a book, on top. It will help blot up more of the stain. Repeat until the stain is gone.

Note: Always test an inconspicuous area first with a bit of the homemade carpet-cleaning solution to ensure colorfastness.

Carpet Stain Removal Guide

- **Candle wax** can be removed by using an ice cube to harden the wax. Then scrape off the wax with a butter knife. Or place a paper bag on top of the wax and use a warmed iron to press down. The bag will soak up the wax. Continue the process until all wax has been removed.
- **Gum:** Use an ice cube to harden the gum, and gradually pick it off.

> The best way to remove any stain is to fight it when it's fresh.

- **General stains:** Fill a spray bottle halfway with white distilled vinegar and then fill the rest with distilled warm water. Spray on the area and blot gently (do not push the stain in). Repeat as necessary.

- **General stains II:** Pour baking soda on the stain to help soak it up. Vacuum away the stain when it's dry.
- **Red wine:** Remove red-wine stains with club soda. Pour on and blot up the stain.

CLOTHING
For removal of clothing stains, check Chapter 15 on laundry.

GENERAL STAINS
- **Heel marks** on floors are easy to remove—just erase them with a pencil eraser!
- **Labels** come off easily—just use a dab of creamy peanut butter on them.
- **Mattresses** that haven't been used in a while can be freshened. Sprinkle with baking soda and let sit overnight. In the morning, vacuum the mattress.
- **Telephones** should be cleaned regularly. Wipe down with rubbing alcohol.
- **Vases** can be cleaned by filling with white vinegar; let the vase sit overnight, and in the morning it should be easy to clean.
- **Wine-stained tablecloths** can be cleaned by laying the stained area over a bowl in the sink. Cover the stain with salt and pour boiling water over the stain. Repeat this process until the stain is gone.

IN THE KITCHEN
- **Burned pots and pans:** A paste of baking soda and water should be scrubbed into the burn and then allowed to sit for an hour or longer. Or try simmering a bit of water with a

generous amount of baking soda on the stove for about five minutes and then turn off the heat and let it sit for an hour before cleaning.

- **Brass** can be cleaned using plain old ketchup! Use a soft cloth to apply and rub it in; then buff it off. Clean tarnished brass by sprinkling on baking soda and then using a lemon on top of that to scrub the stain. It will fizz and clean the tarnish off beautifully.
- **Coffeepots** can get stained over time. Use water, baking-soda paste and a scrubby sponge to get rid of those stubborn stains. Clean out the coffeemaker itself by running a cycle with white vinegar. Pour out the white vinegar and run with fresh water for a few cycles to get rid of the vinegar taste.
- **Coffee stains in cups** can be removed by scrubbing with baking soda or salt. Rinse away and the stain will be gone.
- **Copper pans** can be cleaned with a baking-soda-and-water paste. To remove discolored areas use equal parts salt and white vinegar. Scrub, let sit for twenty minutes, rinse and dry.
- **Electric can openers** can be cleaned by soaking a toothbrush in white vinegar and placing it under the blade and then running the machine.
- **Spot-free glasses:** Drinking glasses will come out spot-free from the dishwasher if you spray them before loading with a mixture of equal parts white vinegar and water.
- **Plastic containers** come clean when scrubbed with baking soda. If it's a stubborn stain, apply a baking-soda-and-water paste and let sit for half an hour. Then scrub it clean.
- **Porcelain** can be cleaned with denture tablets! Let it soak and then scrub the mess away.

- **Sponges or dishcloths** are easily sterilized when cleaned in the dishwasher. Anchor them on the top shelf whenever you're running a load of dishes. You'll never have stinky, unsanitary cleaning sponges or cloths again.
- **Thermos** cleaning is a breeze. Fill with ice, water and a handful of salt and put the lid on. Shake it and then pour out the contents. This method helps remove stubborn coffee and tea stains.
- **Stainless steel utensils** get their old shine back when scrubbed with salt and water.

IN THE BATHROOM

- **Baby shampoo** is an excellent all-around bathroom cleaner!
- **Rust rings** from cans of shaving cream will vanish with a paste made of salt and white vinegar. Apply the paste on the stain, let it sit until dry and then scrub away. To prevent the rings from appearing again, paint the bottom of the can with clear nail polish.
- **Shower doors** come clean with either pure white vinegar or mineral oil.
- **Toilets** can be cleaned easily using a denture-cleaning tablet. Drop one in, let it fizz and then scrub out the toilet. Stubborn stains in toilets can usually be removed with baking soda.
- **Toothpaste** is a good replacement for harsh chemical bathroom tub and tile cleaners. Use a little on a moist sponge. Smells nice, too!

Now that mystery stain that fell from the sky doesn't look quite so challenging! Equipped with the know-how and tools you need to handle stains on clothes, furniture, flooring and more, you'll be a veritable stain-fighting hero. (So that's why you've been wearing those funky red tights. Right? Right. Hey, I don't judge.) Don't let those miserable stains and spots get you down; just deal with them and carry on with the rest of your groovy life. Onward and forward!

Equipped with the know-how and tools, you'll be a veritable stain-fighting hero.

17

Cleaning is a Family Affair

Whether you're a single parent, a huge family of ten, a retired couple or a single happy slob living with a roommate, you need to get your household on board to make your new cleaning routine work. You're not the unpaid cleaning laborer in the home, after all. Everyone has to pitch in to help!

Cleaning bursts are a great way to get your household involved in cleaning. If each family member does a cleaning burst just once every day, you'll get an amazing amount of cleaning accomplished. In a couple weeks, you'll be astounded with how good your home is starting to look.

Young children can spend five minutes cleaning, and older ones can spend up to ten minutes. Keep cleaning bursts and other cleaning tasks reasonable for everyone in your household—you want them to see cleaning as fun, not as punishment. Let's look at some ways to make cleaning a family affair at your house.

THE FAMILY MEETING—HAPPY-SLOB STYLE

Once you've finished reading this book and are ready to implement its ideas in your home, have a family meeting. Share your favorite sections from the book with family members and suggest ways to start doing just one cleaning burst together every day. Ask for everyone's opinion on how to make this new plan work.

Remind them that unlike some cleaning plans, this one is all about balance, and that you're not going to turn into a cleaning warlord. Ask for their opinions on which times work best for cleaning bursts, focus room cleaning and clean-for-alls.

You're not the unpaid cleaning laborer in the home. Everyone has to pitch in.

Ask which tasks they are most interested in and what types of rewards they want to receive for their help.

Make it a fun task by setting up family charts— the kids can get creative with this—and placing stars under each family member's name when they've completed their tasks for the day or week. This really helps everyone get into the fun spirit of these new household cleaning habits, and instead of nagging them, you'll find they'll start doing these tasks on their own. Even sloppy teenagers (hey, I was one of those not all that long ago) will start to appreciate how much better their rooms and living environment are looking.

CLEANING WITH CHILDREN

Only you know the extent to which your children can pitch in with cleaning. Even really young children can help by dusting or sweeping the floors. Not only does it teach them excellent skills, it also helps them feel they're contributing to the household.

Arrange a family cleaning schedule that includes the cleaning bursts and focus rooms for individual family members. The obvious choice is that children's bedrooms will be their focus rooms. Let them know they're responsible for their rooms—and that there are going to be rewards for their efforts. Provide each child with a basic list of cleaning in their room that you want them to do. A list could include tasks such as making their beds every day, keeping the floor clean and putting away their toys. Keep the list as short and simple as possible.

Any efforts your kids make are valuable even if they aren't cleaning pros.

You can assign them additional tasks—such as emptying out the dishwasher and reloading it or keeping the kitchen floor swept. And each child (who is old enough to do so) should put away his or her own laundry.

Work out either how many cleaning tasks your kids will do each day *or* how much time they'll spend. A general guideline could be this: Divide your child's age by two to determine how many tasks they can do a day. An eight-year-old child could handle four tasks, for instance.

If you choose to clean for a set amount of time, keep in mind the age of your child as you assign responsibilities—fifteen minutes for young children could feel like a lifetime to them! About one minute per year of age is the maximum time per day. So an eight-year-old could handle eight minutes. (And, yes, setting a timer for them is very effective.)

And don't turn into a perfectionist now! Any efforts your kids make are valuable, even if they aren't little cleaning pros. If there really is a problem with how they're doing a chore, teach them the right way to do it and then just let them do it. Cleaning side by side is also a nice way to spend time with your kids.

MAKING IT FUN

Whatever amount of time you choose, make cleaning a game by putting on music and dancing around. Laundry tossed into the appropriate baskets is fun when you shoot to score. Dusting is more fun when kids know they can laugh and dance while doing it; put old socks on their hands to do the chore.

Creating Kids' Cleaning Charts

With your child's help, create a cleaning chart that helps them see at a glance what they need to do every day and for the week. Put the cleaning chart on the back of your child's bedroom door and adjust it each week. Apply stars and stickers to the chart when they complete a job.

Especially important is your attitude toward cleaning—if you grumble and groan and do it as if forced at gunpoint, your kids won't have a much more positive view.

Rewards

Cleaning is more fun when everyone gets rewarded for their hard work. Make a trip to the dollar store and pick out a few goodies. Wrap them up and keep them in a reward box. There can be one box for kids and one for adults. Or create a reward jar with folded bits of paper stuffed inside. Each piece should have a reward written on it. Not all rewards have to be items; some should be gifts of your time, such as a trip to the park, an afternoon at the zoo and so on. Kids appreciate your time just as much or more than things you give them. Other rewards might be a day off from any cleaning responsibilities.

Allowances can be adjusted according to household chores completed, too. Let your kids know they'll see nice bonuses in their allowances if they complete all their chores in any given week. You might also create a list of extra chores they can earn bonuses on. If they've been saving their money for something special, they might be happy for the chance to make a bit more money by doing some extra tasks.

Cleaning is more fun when everyone gets rewarded for their hard work.

ELEVEN CLEANING TIPS FOR JUNIOR HAPPY SLOBS

1. **You set the example.** If your kids see you skipping cleaning bursts and grumbling about cleaning, they're not likely going to want to clean either. Be a good example by doing your best to clean with a positive attitude. Make it fun! The more fun cleaning is, the more kids will pick up on that vibe and enjoy themselves.

2. **List it, or they'll resist it.** A list of chores helps kids stay on track with cleaning.

3. **Dust away.** A duster is *way* more appealing to kids than boring old, nasty cleaning rags. Or pop clean socks on each of their hands.

4. **Squirt, squirt.** Nontoxic cleaners make cleaning fun for kids because they get to squirt stuff. Who doesn't like squirting stuff? Provide kids with cleaning rags to wipe it up.

5. **Rich rewards.** Reward kids' efforts. These mini rewards keep kids on track with their new cleaning plan. See page 178 for more reward ideas.

6. **Mini cleaning kits for kids.** You have a cleaning kit for yourself, so now that your kids are getting in on the cleaning action you'll want to create kits for them, too. Large plastic milk jugs are perfect for this. Just cut off the top section, leaving the handle intact. Fill with a bottle or two of nontoxic or homemade cleaners, a few rags, a duster—whichever supplies they need to fulfill their duties around the home. Provide only nontoxic cleaners so your kids will be safe.

7. **Stowaways.** Make it easier for your kids to keep their rooms clean by providing adequate storage. If your child is a bookworm, and yet has nowhere to stash treasured tomes, it isn't

possible keep their room tidy. You can buy funky, colorful storage containers and bookshelves especially for kids. Add some labels so children always know where to stow their stuff. For young children who can't read yet, make picture labels—pictures of sports equipment, toys, etc.—to help them understand what goes where.

8. **Take time to teach.** Make sure your children understand how to complete a task before you assign it. Show them how each task is done beforehand, and always thank them for their efforts after they're finished.

9. **The early bird gets the...vacuum?** Start kids at a young age to help with housecleaning. They're naturally curious and want to pitch in, and habits learned early on are most likely to stick and become lifelong ones. Get your kids in on the cleaning act as soon as they can hold a duster.

10. **Just start, already!** The best plans and ideas are going to fail if you never implement them. So while it helps your kids to have cleaning supplies at the ready and a worksheet of tasks for them to do, it won't help if you get so bogged down in the details you never begin at all! Get them started on a task a day, and then add to it from there, keeping it reasonable so they aren't burdened with too much work for their age.

11. **Keep it simple.** Keep chores simple for kids, especially young children. Don't aggravate them with tasks beyond their comprehension.

Cleaning with kids and family members can be one of life's great challenges—or you can turn it around on its nose and make it a lot of fun. (That'll keep them guessing, now, won't it?) Keep these tips and hints in mind when you encourage your family to get involved in the cleaning. Remember, don't expect perfection (and don't nag); praise your family for what they accomplish, and work together to get the house a bit cleaner and a lot more comfortable. Wow, this cleaning jazz could actually turn into some pretty efficient family-bonding time, when you think about it.

18
Furbusters! Cleaning for Pet Owners

Living with pets is a joy! But cleaning after them isn't always quite as much fun. Pet messes can run the gamut from litter-box "misses" to mucky aquariums and puppy blunders of the pooey kind. Not to mention the fur they leave behind. Animal lovers take comfort: This chapter will provide you with the tips you need to clean up after your beloved pals.

LITTER-BOX CLEANING 101

I am the proud mom—oops, I mean owner—of two adorable cats. One is an outspoken and devoted black-and-white kitty of undeterminable heritage, while the other is a calico-Siamese mix who has a sweet temperament and is blessedly quiet, if not a bit timid. (She's currently curled up near me, deep asleep and looking so adorable as to provide great motivation for this chapter!) So litter-box cleaning is a daily affair here. I've learned the hard way what works and what doesn't.

What works is scoopable litter! (Check the sidebar below for fabulous new options that are healthier for your pet and the environment.) This marvelous stuff makes the task of cleaning kitty litter a breeze. Most likely you already use scoopable litter if you're a cat owner. If not, you'll definitely want to give this a try. Veterinarians suggest gradually adding a little scoopable litter to your cats' current litter, giving them a chance to adjust to the different feel of it. Eventually you can just replace it completely.

I keep a stash of biodegradable bags (found at my local pet store) near the litter box, along with plenty of fresh, clean litter, a great big box of baking soda and, of course, the scoop. Every time you change the litter, be sure to get out every little bit of waste and chuck it out right away. Sprinkle the remaining litter generously with baking soda and then top with fresh litter. Using the scoop, give it a bit of a stir so the baking soda mixes with all the litter. Voilà! Lovely, clean litter for your cats. The baking soda is very effective at reducing odors.

Every month or so, you can empty the litter box completely

Lovelier Litter

Your local pet shop carries new varieties of litter that are better for your pet and planet Earth. With a wide new range including corncob litter, newspaper litter, pine litter—and even biodegradable types that allow you to scoop and flush directly into the toilet—you have many from which to choose. Your pets will thank you because the clay in traditional litters can cause digestive or respiratory problems. And these new litters leave behind less of an environmental "footprint" when you use them. So new litters are definitely worth investigating!

and give it a good, thorough scrub, using just a little mild soap and hot water. Rinse until all remnants of soap are gone and then dry thoroughly before refilling with fresh litter. You can add a little white vinegar to the soapy water when cleaning to add disinfecting and odor-neutralizing power.

Don't use bleach—the ammonia in bleach smells like cat urine to kitties. Plus, it's too strong a cleaner for their sensitive little noses, and it can wreak havoc on their health.

> *Don't use bleach—the ammonia in bleach smells like cat urine to kitties.*

MUDDY PAW PATROL...AND OTHER CLEANING TIPS FOR DOG OWNERS

Pooches just returned from their daily walks inevitably bring mud and dirt into the home. For just that reason, keep a moistened sponge near the door and wipe puppy's paws as soon as he comes inside. For the very same reason, keep a pile of old towels handy for wiping off your buddy when he's been in the elements—rain, snow, sleet or, of course, that irresistible puddle!

For dog owners, one of the greatest cleaning chores you do is one that isn't even contained in your house—we're talking poop-scoopin' action! You can find wonderful biodegradable or compostable doggy poop-scoop bags at any good pet store. In a pinch, recycled brown paper lunch bags will do the trick. (In the store near my home, I can buy one hundred of them for just a couple bucks.) Choose these over plastic bags, which will sit in a landfill for a very long time before ever beginning to break down.

FUR, FUR, EVERYWHERE!

Ah, the constant battle against our furry friends' shedding. Obviously, vacuuming on a more regular basis becomes more important for us happy slobs with pets. Another great way to remove fur from furniture is to don a rubber glove, slightly moistened, and run it along the surface of the furniture. It helps the fur ball up, and then you can remove it. Clothing brushes and sticky roller-type brushes also help remove fur from furniture and clothes. (I've found that using regular old masking tape works well, too. Just apply strips of it and pull it, and the fur comes right along with it!)

Brushing your pets on a daily basis helps greatly reduce the amount of fur lying about in your home. Some pets come to absolutely love this and see it as a fun daily treat. It's healthier for your pets, too, as it reduces the amount of fur they ingest while grooming themselves.

White Vinegar Stops the Scratching!

If your cats are scratching the furniture, use whole-strength white vinegar to deter them. Just dab a little on the areas they're scratching and repeat as necessary. The cats will not appreciate the full-strength odor and will gradually stop their scratchy actions.

FEEDING AREAS

Another area of concern for pet owners is the feeding area where our furry little pals chow down. Let's just say that most pets aren't exactly up to par on their dining manners, so there's often a mucky mess left behind. Here are some tips for keeping the area tidier.

- Keep a plastic place mat beneath the food and water dishes. It makes cleanup easier. One friend told me she uses a rubber bath mat because the suction cups help keep the mat securely in place.
- Sweep or vacuum the area often.
- Don't use bleach or ammonia cleaners around any areas where pets spend time. It smells like urine to them, and they'll likely turn the area into their own personal toilet!
- Keep food dishes cleaned out regularly, using only a tiny bit of very mild soap and warm water. Make sure to rinse out very well before refilling with the food and water.

SMALL PETS

I grew up with a whole lineage of hamsters named Hamlet. (I couldn't get my head around a cuter name for a hamster than that. If I had a hamster again today, I'd likely still call him or her Hamlet.) Small pets such as hamsters, guinea pigs and mice require regular cage changes. Fresh pine shavings smell lovely, and if you change their cage bedding every week, your pets will be happier and healthier. Remember to sweep around the cage often, too, as it gets to be a bit of a mess when they scratch around and in the process scatter shavings all over the place.

If there's odor coming from your small pets (such as mice, hamsters, gerbils, guinea pigs and rabbits), it's likely dirty cage bedding

Black and White vs. Technicolor

Did you know some colored newspaper inks contain toxins? To be safe, use only black-and-white newsprint to cover the bottom of your birdcages.

is the real culprit. Change the cage bedding every week to ensure happy, healthy little pets. They'll certainly appreciate it, and your home will stay fresher and neater at the same time.

AQUARIUM CLEANING

A stinky fish tank or other aquarium for lizards or snakes can get really nasty looking and smelling if it isn't properly maintained. Any reputable pet store can teach you how to properly care for these pets and the aquarium they live in.

Keep it as clean as possible—for your enjoyment and definitely for the health of your pets. But check with aquarium experts before you go cleaning crazy. Some algae and bacteria are actually incredibly good for your pets and work as little filtering systems to naturally clean out waste from the water. You definitely want to check with the pros who know—and then invest in a manual about caring for fish or reptiles to fully understand how to clean their homes properly.

FINEST FEATHERED FRIENDS

Pet birds bring joy and musicality to the lives of their owners, so show how much you appreciate them by learning the basics of cage cleaning.

- **Load up on layers:** Layers of newspaper on the bottom of your birds' cages will make daily liner cleaning much easier. On "light use" days, you can simply remove the first couple layers of newspaper to reveal fresh, clean newspaper underneath without going to the trouble of replacing all the newspapers. Just make sure that droppings or water didn't saturate through to other layers so that a truly fresh layer of paper is available on the top.
- **Deep clean that cage:** Depending on the type of birds, number of birds and even the size of the birds you have, you'll need to do a thorough cleaning of the cage anywhere from every week to every month. This involves removing your feathered friend(s) to another location and then removing everything in the cage—including food and water dishes and hard toys. Everything should get a good scrub in a hot, soapy water mixture—the inside of the cage, the dishes, the hard toys. Make sure to rinse water and food dishes very well and dry equally well before returning them to the cage to be refilled. (Even slightly moist food dishes can make for moldy food.)

Scrubby Tools for Cleaning Cages

A good soak in that hot, soapy water mixture will often dislodge bits of food or waste that have hardened. Otherwise try light sanding paper, an old toothbrush (which you likely already have in your cleaning kit anyway!) or a scrubby cleaning pad. Any or all should help greatly with those down-and-dirty cage-cleaning tasks.

ODOR CONTROL

We love our pets for their devotion to us and definitely for how they make us laugh with their crazy antics. But their stinky odor is not quite so endearing. Here are some ways to keep pet odors to a minimum at your house:

- Regularly bathe your pets. Ask your veterinarian for tips if your pet hates baths and makes such a fuss so as to make bathing it impossible.
- If you have cats, clean the litter every day. Add baking soda, as suggested above, to absorb more odors.
- Doggy bad breath got you down? New breath-control biscuits (and even breath mints!) are treats your pooch will love, and they will make him more pleasant to be around. If chronic bad breath is a problem for your pooch, be sure to advise his vet. Sometimes this can be a warning sign of an underlying health condition.
- Neutralizing odors in small pets' cages is easy. First and foremost, keep the cage clean by changing the bedding every week. A sprinkling of baking soda beneath the bedding will naturally soak up even more odors, and it's a natural and safe option for your pets.
- Scented cat litter and shavings might seem like a happy slob's dream come true, but they're not as sweet as they might seem at first smell. Artificial scents can harm your pets' health, so instead choose unscented, pure products. Besides, the best way to zap odors in the first place is by maintaining a clean cage or litter box.
- Aquariums and tanks can be odor free with the help of a specially designed product made for just that purpose. At

your pet store, ask about natural aquarium deodorizers that help get rid of any nasty smells you'd rather not have in your home. The staff should be able to help you find just what you're looking for.

Our favorite little critters (sorry, I mean *pet companions*) add a lot of heart to our homes, along with copious amounts of poo, hair balls and other hairy contributions! But they really are our dear pals, so knowing some much-needed techniques to cope with pet messes will help us love them all the more. Now if only we could equip them with little cleaning pads on their paws...they'd be even more useful! Until then, we'll just conquer the cleaning on our own.

Conclusion: Cleaner, Happier Homes

Now even we happy slobs can have cleaner homes without trying to reach some unattainable goal of perfection (aka sterilization). Using the *No-Hassle Housecleaning* guide, you can reach a satisfactory level of cleanliness in your home. Just remember the 3-Step Solution whenever you're feeling bogged down with housecleaning chores:

- Two cleaning bursts every day (five to fifteen minutes each)
- A focus room every day for about ten minutes
- One clean for all per week

It's not complicated, and the silly system actually works! I don't expect you to become a neat freak. I don't *want* you to become a neat freak! I want you to maintain your cool, stylish, happy-slob attitude but realize at the same time that your life at home will be less stressful if you implement these few simple steps. No sweat. Well, a bit of sweat is involved when we're cleaning, but let's call it cardio.

Just remember to keep cleaning simple and don't stress, and you'll be shocked at how even happy slobs like us can reduce the mess in our homes. You'll clean, you'll conquer and then you'll carry on with your life. Happy cleaning to you, my friends!

The Happy Slob's 25 Favorite Cleaning Tips

1. **All-purpose cleaner is a snap to make!** Add a couple squirts of mild dishwashing liquid to a spray bottle and fill with water. Shake gently and use as you would any cleaner. Another happy-slob favorite is one part white vinegar added to three parts water. White vinegar is a natural mold killer, disinfectant and cleaner, so buy it in huge bottles and use it instead of harsh commercial products.

2. **Baking soda is our best friend!** You can use it in place of harsh commercial powder cleansers, as a natural odor absorber for stinky spots like kitty-litter boxes and as a simple baking-soda-and-water paste (add a bit of dishwashing liquid soap if you like) to make a fantastic bathroom cleaner.

3. **P.A.Y.** P.A.Y. means pick up after yourself! It sounds silly and obvious, but one way to reduce clutter and maintain a tidier home is to put things away as soon as you're finished with them. It takes only a few seconds and will greatly reduce your cleaning time.

4. ***Pick a corner, any corner.*** To start cleaning a room, that is. Pick one corner of the room and start there, working in one continuous direction until you're done. You won't be wasting time running around the room aimlessly.

5. ***Brooms*** pick up more dust when you occasionally spray a little furniture polish on the bottom of the bristles. It also helps keep dirt from sticking to the bristles.

6. ***Cleaning kits*** can be made from any container, such as a cleaning bucket or toolbox. It's easier to clean when you have everything you need at hand.

7. ***Frugal Fabric Softener I:*** Use a cup of white vinegar in the wash when you'd normally add fabric softener. The strong vinegar smell will be gone by the time the wash is done, and you'll be impressed by how the vinegar softens clothes and reduces static electricity.

8. ***Frugal Fabric Softener II:*** Use diluted hair conditioner! Water it down—about one part conditioner to three parts water—and use about ¼ cup at a time. This obviously won't be your everyday fabric softener, but it's a great option if you've suddenly run out and need to run a load of laundry, pronto.

9. ***Laundry detergent replacement.*** Use a capful or two of shampoo. It cleans well and is also an excellent stain remover. Just don't overdo it, or you might have a bubble-bath scenario all over the laundry room floor.

10. **Ring around the collar.** Remove that nasty stain from shirt collars with a bit of liquid laundry detergent or shampoo rubbed into the stain. Let it sit for an hour or so before laundering in the hottest water that is safe for the fabric.

11. **Club soda** makes your sinks and appliances shine. Just use that old bottle that's been sitting forever at the back of the refrigerator.

12. **Pan degunking.** A little overeager when you baked that lasagna? Nasty, baked-on gunk can be removed with a fabric-softener sheet! Add a sheet, fill the pan with water and let it sit overnight. In the morning it should clean up easily. (Note: Use this trick only on stainless or glass baking dishes. The fabric-softener sheet might actually damage or even remove nonstick surface treatments, so don't use it on any nonstick surface.)

13. **Plastic container stains** can be removed with a paste of baking soda and water scrubbed into the stain and then washed as usual.

14. **Stainless steel polisher.** If the dishwasher isn't getting your utensils shiny clean, scrub with a bit of salt mixed with water to make a thick paste. Rinse and they should sparkle. For stainless appliances, a tiny bit of olive oil on a cleaning cloth will buff up those appliances and get all the fingerprints and smudges off.

15. **Rinse-agent substitute.** You guessed it: more vinegar! Fill your dishwasher's rinse-agent compartment with vinegar. Works fantastically well! (And, of course, it's so much cheaper.) Either plain white vinegar or apple-cider vinegar will work just fine for this.

16.   *Rubbing alcohol* makes stainless steel sinks, faucets and kitchen appliances shine. Just use a little on the sponge as a final buff-up if you're really trying to impress someone. What a smooth (and shiny) happy slob you are!

17.   *Garbage disposals.* Throw a few handfuls of ice and a chopped lemon into the disposal about once month. The ice sharpens the blades, and the lemon deodorizes the disposal and leaves a wonderful scent.

18.   *Clog remover.* Pour one cup of baking soda down a clogged drain, followed by one cup of white vinegar. Let it sit for fifteen to twenty minutes and then flush with plenty of boiling water. Doing this every week or two will help prevent nasty clogs from occurring in the first place. Don't use this solution if you have recently used a commercial clog remover, and never combine this solution with a commercial clog remover.

19.   *Shower cleaning* is a breeze if you keep a scrubby sponge or scrub brush in the shower and give the shower a quick cleaning while your conditioner is doing its work. Do this every time you shower, and you've erased the entire chore of slavishly scrubbing the bath and shower.

20.   *Shower-curtain cleaning.* Ick, what is that growing on your fashionable shower curtain? Try a teaspoon of tea-tree oil in a cup of plain water, spray it on and let sit. Don't rinse. Or mix ½ cup white vinegar with ½ cup water and spray it on. Rinse off with water. Shower curtains can also be washed by tossing them into the washing machine with a couple towels.

21. **Shower doors** are easy to clean—use straight white vinegar to cut right through the buildup of soap scum. Mineral oil also does a good job. Rinse with water after cleaning. Doing this regularly will help reduce the buildup.

22. **Showerheads** get unclogged and run smoothly again when you pour some white vinegar in a heavy-duty plastic storage bag and tie it around the showerhead so the entire showerhead is immersed. Tie securely with a twist tie or use some duct tape. (Alternate: You can remove the showerhead and let it sit in a bowl of white vinegar.) Let it sit at least fifteen minutes.

23. **Bathtub cleaning.** Inexpensive bubble baths or baby shampoos are unexpectedly good bathroom cleaners. Just a bit on a sponge works and smells great.

24. **Toilet cleaning** is a snap when you drop a denture-cleaning tab into the throne. Give it a scrub with a toilet brush and flush it all away.

25. **Toilet brushes.** Keep one behind every toilet in the home. It's one of those icky things you don't want to tote around with you. Replace it often.

Focus-Room Cleaning Chart

This is a fairly exhaustive list of cleaning tasks that can be performed in your home. Blank spaces are provided so you can list specific tasks unique to your living space. This should provide inspiration on what you can accomplish during your focus-room cleanings. Try to do different cleaning tasks during each focus-room cleaning to get your home cleaned more thoroughly over time.

BATHROOM

- ☐ **Cabinets:** Wipe down outside. Remove everything from inside, wipe down, declutter and then replace.
- ☐ **Countertops:** Wipe down.
- ☐ **Countertops:** Declutter, clean toothbrush holder, lotion dispenser.
- ☐ **Light fixtures:** Dust.
- ☐ **Light switches:** Disinfect.
- ☐ **Medicine cabinet:** Wipe down outside. Clear out old products, wipe down shelves and then restock.

- ☐ *Mirror:* Clean.
- ☐ *Sink:* Clean and polish faucets.
- ☐ *Toilet:* Clean interior bowl, lid and seat, and wipe down entire exterior.
- ☐ *Tub and shower:* Clean the tub. Scrub the tile and grout lines (unless you do the "Never Clean the Shower Again" method, see page 126, which will eliminate this task).
- ☐ *Tub and shower:* Clean bath mat.
- ☐ *Tub and shower:* Wash shower curtain.
- ☐ *Flooring:* Sweep and mop or vacuum.
- ☐ _____
- ☐ _____
- ☐ _____
- ☐ _____
- ☐ _____
- ☐ _____

LIVING AREAS/FAMILY ROOMS

- ☐ *Curtains or blinds:* Dust or wash (check manufacturer's cleaning suggestions for curtains—they may need to be dry-cleaned).
- ☐ *Fireplace:* Clean/dust outside.
- ☐ *Flooring:* Sweep and mop or vacuum. Wash rugs.
- ☐ *Mantel:* Dust. Also dust knickknacks or photos. Declutter.
- ☐ _____
- ☐ _____
- ☐ _____
- ☐ _____
- ☐ _____
- ☐ _____

KITCHEN

- [ ] **Cupboards:** Throw out old food and organize inside.
- [ ] **Cupboards:** Wipe down outside.
- [ ] **Dishwasher:** Wipe down outside. Occasionally run a load with white vinegar to clean the inside.
- [ ] **Flooring:** Sweep and mop.
- [ ] **Refrigerator:** Clean drip pan beneath appliance. Occasionally vacuum back coils.
- [ ] **Refrigerator (exterior):** Wipe down and declutter.
- [ ] **Refrigerator (interior):** Clean out old food. Wipe out.
- [ ] **Refrigerator (interior):** Replace box of baking soda to freshen.
- [ ] **Freezer:** Clean out old food or freezer-burned food and defrost as needed.
- [ ] **Light fixtures:** Dust.
- [ ] **Light switches:** Disinfect.
- [ ] **Microwave:** Wipe down outside. Clean interior.
- [ ] **Pantry:** Remove old food items. Wipe down shelves and reorganize.
- [ ] **Sink:** Scrub inside sink. Polish outside and taps.
- [ ] **Stove (interior):** Clean inside the oven.
- [ ] **Stove (exterior):** Wipe down and clean drip pans.
- [ ] **Stove vent and filter:** Clean.
- [ ] **Trash compactor:** Clean inside and out.
- [ ] _____
- [ ] _____
- [ ] _____
- [ ] _____
- [ ] _____
- [ ] _____

BEDROOMS

- ☐ **Bed:** Change bedding.
- ☐ **Bed:** Wipe down headboard, etc.
- ☐ **Closets:** Declutter.
- ☐ **Dressers:** Dust or wipe down outside. Declutter drawers and reorganize.
- ☐ **Dust surfaces.**
- ☐ **Kids' rooms:** Put away toys in storage containers.
- ☐ **Laundry:** Put dirty clothes in laundry hamper or take to laundry room.
- ☐ **Mirrors:** Clean.
- ☐ **Shelving and storage:** Declutter and reorganize. Dust.
- ☐ **Flooring:** Sweep and mop or vacuum.
- ☐ _____
- ☐ _____
- ☐ _____
- ☐ _____
- ☐ _____
- ☐ _____

CLOSETS

- ☐ **Declutter and reorganize shelf by shelf.**
- ☐ _____
- ☐ _____
- ☐ _____
- ☐ _____
- ☐ _____
- ☐ _____

DINING ROOM

- ☐ *Buffet and hutch or china cabinet:* Dust and occasionally polish.
- ☐ *Dining room table:* Wipe down (occasionally polish with wood polish).
- ☐ *Flooring:* Sweep and mop or vacuum.
- ☐ _____
- ☐ _____
- ☐ _____
- ☐ _____

LAUNDRY AND UTILITY ROOM

- ☐ *Countertops:* Wipe down.
- ☐ *Declutter/put away clean clothes.*
- ☐ *Washer and drier:* Wipe down outside.
- ☐ *Flooring:* Sweep and mop.
- ☐ _____
- ☐ _____
- ☐ _____
- ☐ _____

GARAGE

- ☐ *Declutter* by having a garage sale!
- ☐ *Flooring:* Sweep.
- ☐ *Sporting goods:* Declutter and reorganize.
- ☐ *Tools:* Organize.
- ☐ _____
- ☐ _____
- ☐ _____
- ☐ _____

HOME OFFICE

- ☐ **Computers:** Dust monitor. Wipe down keyboard with disinfectant wipes.
- ☐ **Desk:** Declutter. File papers. Wipe down surfaces.
- ☐ **Office equipment (faxes, printers):** Wipe down.
- ☐ **Shelves:** Declutter books and reorganize. Dust.
- ☐ **Telephones:** Wipe with disinfectant wipes.
- ☐ _____
- ☐ _____
- ☐ _____
- ☐ _____
- ☐ _____
- ☐ _____

ENTRY AND HALLWAYS

- ☐ **Back door:** Wash inside and outside (including any windows).
- ☐ **Flooring:** Sweep and mop.
- ☐ **Front door:** Wash inside and outside (including any windows).
- ☐ **Hallway storage units:** Declutter and dust.
- ☐ **Light fixtures:** Dust.
- ☐ _____
- ☐ _____
- ☐ _____
- ☐ _____
- ☐ _____
- ☐ _____

WINDOWS

- ☐ *Curtain rods:* Dust.
- ☐ *Exterior windows:* Clean.
- ☐ *Interior windows:* Clean.
- ☐ *Wipe down screens.*
- ☐ *Wipe down tracks.*
- ☐ _____
- ☐ _____
- ☐ _____
- ☐ _____

OTHER AREAS IN YOUR HOME

- ☐ _____
- ☐ _____
- ☐ _____
- ☐ _____
- ☐ _____
- ☐ _____
- ☐ _____
- ☐ _____
- ☐ _____

Index

Books of Interest

Organize Now!

This book offers practical, action-oriented advice that teaches you how to organize any part of your life in less than one week. Quick, easy-to-follow checklists let you spend more time organizing and less time reading—a perfect fit for your busy lifestyle! ISBN-13: 978-1-60061-108-7; ISBN-10: 1-60061-108-7; hardcover with concealed spiral, 240 pages, #Z2100.

The Housewife's Handbook

You'll find all the hints, secrets and tips you'll ever need to run a modern home in *The Housewife's Handbook.* From folding sheets to tackling lime scale in baths and basins to unblocking drains to defrosting the freezer, this book has it all. ISBN-13: 978-1-55870-875-4; ISBN-10: 1-55870-875-8; paperback, 352 pages, #Z3229.

Go Organize!

Go Organize! will transform your views of organizing and put you on a path to stay organized for the rest of your life. You'll learn how to organize every room in your home with a simple three-step process. ISBN-13: 978-1-55870-889-1; ISBN-10: 1-55870-889-8; paperback, 240 pages, #Z4225.

These books and other fine F+W Media titles are available at your local bookstore or from online suppliers.